UNIVERSITY PRESS OF FLORIDA

Florida A&M University, Tallahassee
Florida Atlantic University, Boca Raton
Florida Gulf Coast University, Ft. Myers
Florida International University, Miami
Florida State University, Tallahassee
New College of Florida, Sarasota
University of Central Florida, Orlando
University of Florida, Gainesville
University of North Florida, Jacksonville
University of South Florida, Tampa
University of West Florida, Pensacola

UNIVERSITY PRESS OF FLORIDA

Gainesville/Tallahassee/Tampa/Boca Raton
Pensacola/Orlando/Miami/Jacksonville/Ft. Myers/Sarasota

So, You Want
to Be a
Ballet Dancer?

SECOND EDITION

Jennifer Carlynn Kronenberg
Principal Dancer, Miami City Ballet

Foreword by Edward Villella
Founding Artistic Director, Miami City Ballet

BALANCHINE is a Trademark of The George Balanchine Trust.
All images of dances are courtesy of The George Balanchine Trust

FIGURE 1. (*frontis*) Pas de Deux from George Balanchine's *Agon*.
© The George Balanchine Trust, photo courtesy of Joe Gato.

18 17 16 15 14 13   6 5 4 3 2 1

A record of cataloging-in-publication data is available from the Library of Congress.

ISBN 978-0-8130-4480-4

University Press of Florida
15 Northwest 15th Street
Gainesville, FL 32611-2079
http://www.upf.com

I lovingly dedicate this book to all the wonderful students whom I have had the joy of teaching over the years; to Teresa Aubel, my first teacher and mentor, who committed herself unconditionally to helping me make my dreams come true; to Edward Villella, who has shaped me into the artist that I've become and instilled a new dimension of thought and understanding in my dancing; to my late grandmother, Carla Zieglersky, who continuously gave me the strength to reach for the stars; and last but certainly most significant, to my loving husband Carlos Miguel Guerra, who supported and encouraged me through this entire process and made me truly believe that I could, and should, write this book.

Contents

Foreword

I can divide my life into two distinct periods: before and after my exposure to ballet. Before ballet, I was a feisty kid with an abundance of physicality from a blue-collar community—Bayside, Queens. I channeled my physicality into sandlot baseball and street and schoolyard activities. My sister was off taking ballet lessons when I was knocked unconscious by a baseball. When she came home with our mother, I was told that I could not be trusted on the streets anymore and I would have to accompany them to my sister's ballet lessons. I was *made* to take lessons. I was humiliated and embarrassed. I was seven.

After six months I began to like it; then I was hooked. It was to me now such a superior physicality. Subsequently, when I was sixteen, my sister quit, so my father sent me to a military college where I won my letters in baseball and was a welterweight boxing champion. I desperately missed ballet, however, and when I graduated four years later, I presented myself to the New York City Ballet. George Balanchine invited me to join his company, and there I had my first serious exposure to ballet and a different *kind* of physicality. What I experienced and learned there utterly transformed my life; I discovered a mind-driven physicality—*dance*—what Balanchine called "the poetry of gesture." Once that discovery crossed my horizon, my life was unalterably changed . . . and I never looked back.

Edward Villella
Founding Artistic Director, Miami City Ballet

Preface

During her childhood, almost every little girl will become enraptured by the dream of becoming a ballerina, just like I did. For most, the thought of being an enchanted swan princess dressed in a gorgeous tutu, dancing round and round to beautiful music on the delicate tips of her toes, is truly captivating. The life of a ballerina seems so perfect and entirely magical, but is it really so? For some, yes. For others, unexpected challenges may eventually outweigh the rewards.

I became smitten with ballet years ago, and I am one of a few fortunate enough to have had my dream turned into my reality. For the most part, life dealt me a good hand, and for that I am ever grateful. The road to my success was far from smooth, however, and the bumps continued even once I was accepted into a professional company. The amount of work, the pressure (mostly self-imposed), and the angst, sweat, and tears that I found myself enduring were greater than I'd ever imagined. I came to understand that for a real ballerina, everything is not always "beautiful at the ballet."

I have learned to take on and overcome so many obstacles and I have truly enjoyed this extremely elite and fulfilling career, despite the occasional hardship. Dancing has become as essential to my being as eating, sleeping, and breathing. I will always be a dancer inside, even when my career as a ballerina comes to an end. The magic, the music, and my sheer love of the art will never die. The "red shoes" in me will surely keep on dancing forever. After working my hardest to reap the rewards that this career has to offer, I am now in a prime position to provide useful advice to the next generation of dancers embarking on their own adventures in today's ballet world, and to their parents; advice I wish I'd had when I began my journey.

Years of dancing professionally with Miami City Ballet and frequent additional engagements as both a teacher and guest artist have enlightened me to just how many young dancers lack knowledge of basic pre-professional skills and etiquette. Many don't fully understand what striving to be a professional truly entails.

Not every child who has the ballet "itch" is destined to become a professional. It is an extremely specialized art requiring a unique discipline and dedication, and it is often very subjective. Some figure this out for themselves rather quickly; others are let down the hard way. Blunt rejection can be hurtful (but does not necessarily mean that one won't ever dance!). I didn't have a big sister or an older friend in the professional ballet world to counsel me on the ups and downs I would have to endure. I'd like to take on the role of that friend and big sister to all the young dancers who make countless sacrifices and dedicate hours to practice each day in the hope of making it.

I hope that in sharing my experiences and acquired knowledge of the profession, this book will serve as a comforting companion to students and young professionals alike; as a tool and a reference to which they can really relate. Crazy high-jinx, mishaps, and all, I once went through the same challenges that many may find overwhelming, and in spite of it all, my journey did lead to a fantastically successful career.

Ballet is a world of regality, beauty, and artistry; both welcoming and somewhat intimidating. I'd like to let students, their parents, and young professionals catch a unique glimpse through my eyes into the professional world; a sneak peek in on what may yet be to come. My goal is to empower the next generation of dancers and help them to enjoy each fleeting moment of this amazing career to the fullest, just as they should.

1

Turning Inspiration into Perspiration

Choosing the Right School—Ballet and Academics

I've always imagined becoming a ballerina, from as far back as I can clearly remember. I truly cherished the thought of wearing a glittering tiara and dancing around in a beautiful pink tutu. I think the ballet bug bit me hardest at around six years old. The PBS channel was often playing on our living room television, and anytime a ballet came on I was completely entranced; almost hypnotized. Little by little I would try to mimic the steps; I just couldn't sit still. I'd feel the music swell inside me, and bursting at the seams I would dance around everywhere. I danced at home, at school, at my grandma's house, even in the streets.

The itch just would not subside, and when I turned seven my parents enrolled me in classes at a local ballet school. I was immediately insistent upon attending classes every day, but understandably, my mother proceeded with caution. How could she possibly have imagined how serious I was? Maybe I wouldn't be able to handle the long classes and the discipline. She assumed that once the initial excitement wore off, I would eventually get bored.

I began my lessons once a week, which quickly turned into twice, then three times. I'd come home with the steps that eluded me written down in a small notebook. I was determined to figure them out (the mechanics of a *jeté entrelacé*—a jump where the legs appear to be interlaced, were especially difficult). Hidden in my room, I would practice the steps tirelessly, over and over again. Within a couple of months my parents began sending me to class every day.

I felt exhilarated; I immediately knew that this was what I wanted to do forever. The movements themselves were perfectly precise, and I adored listening to the beautiful classical music. The harmonious pairing of the two created an overwhelming excitement that swelled inside me. It was an immediate passion that I still find difficult to explain. I had truly found my niche, but I was still very young. Understandably again, my parents were prepared for me gradually to lose interest. I suppose they assumed that I would one day give it up to be with friends, get sick of the discipline, or eventually yearn to study something else.

At first it's great fun; but as classes advance, they become more strictly regimented. For many, ballet lessons can become a chore, but I didn't mind. The more I trained, the more I fell in love with it. Fortunately I had a teacher who was knowledgeable, nurturing, and extremely inspirational: Teresa Aubel. She took her craft *very* seriously. To those who were strictly dedicated and willing to work, she would offer the world. This is a phenomenal exchange for someone envisioning a career, but selling one's soul to ballet does not appeal to everyone. Some just want to dance for fun, as a hobby. While this is perfectly normal and justifiable, anyone falling into that category would have felt suffocated in such a hard-working and serious environment.

A child's first teacher has the ability either to inspire dreams and creativity or to crush them. If a young child's first taste of ballet is a bitter one, the child may not want to continue to higher levels of training. Each school is different, some rigid and discipline oriented and others more liberal, focusing primarily on movement and creativity. The one to choose depends almost entirely on the child and the willingness to commit. Parents should be sure to observe a few classes with their child at any prospective school. *Are the classes initially appealing to the child? Does he or she exhibit interest in participating within that environment?* Parents should also confirm that they themselves are comfortable with the teaching techniques of any particular teacher or school before committing their child to a series of classes.

In the beginning and intermediate years of training it may be in a student's best interests either to study at a smaller school or to choose a larger school offering intimate class sizes. The environment in small schools is usually more nurturing, and greater attention can be paid to each individual student. Similar benefits may just as easily be found in large schools, provided the class size is not overwhelming. I have found that when younger children train primarily with one teacher they quickly build trust and familiarity through the learning process, while avoiding the confusion of potentially conflicting stylistic and technical demands. Later, as students advance, they reap greater benefit from being introduced to various teachers and methods. Attending workshops, summer intensives, or guest teachers' master classes at one's home studio are all great ways to gain experience, knowledge, and stylistic variety.

During the preteen or early teenage years, if a student seems truly serious about pursuing a career in ballet, enrolling in a prominent "professional" school where auditions are required for acceptance may be the way to go. In these types of academies the students are immersed in a more competitive atmosphere where their training can be further advanced. Class schedules are surely intensified, sometimes even mimicking a professional company schedule. In this sort of setting students will likely get an accurate idea of what lies ahead of them—at least as far as competition, standards, and demands are concerned. They will be inclined to develop a realistic perspective about their capabilities and weaknesses in comparison to others of their age and level of training.

Prominent schools, often affiliated with professional companies, may also open doors to professional opportunities. Students should keep in mind, though, that making the leap to a more serious school usually necessitates sacrificing in other areas of life. They may find they have less free time for social activities, they are surrounded by increased competitiveness, and they get less personal attention and feel more pressured to succeed. Class schedules may also interfere with traditional school hours, introducing the controversial subject of home schooling and correspondence course alternatives; not the best routes for everyone. These life choices should be discussed thoroughly with family and teachers before arriving at a decision. At my parents' suggestion, I chose to stay enrolled in a public high school throughout my training. I remained a full-time academic student straight through to high school graduation. This provided me a more conventional educational routine, allowed me the benefits of a mainstream social life, and gave my parents general peace of mind. As much as I enjoyed my school, it also took its toll on me. Had I not been the disciplined teenager I was, I would surely have burned out. School plus homework, extra study, ballet, and commuting made for very long days and short nights and became a tremendous burden to bear. Nevertheless, it was an experience that I would not trade for the world. It ultimately played an essential role in my coming of age.

Home schooling and correspondence courses are the most popular alternatives to conventional schooling. In this approach to education a student is usually taught at home by a parent or professional tutor, making scheduling quite flexible. In some correspondence situations a student self-teaches, with the assistance of prepared lesson plans, books, and online classes. In this case there is normally a phone number or online internet forum provided; a help line of sorts. For this method of education to be effective and worthwhile, a student must be extremely self-motivated and disciplined.

There are both pros and cons to home schooling, just as

there are with mainstream education. With increased scheduling flexibility, serious ballet students have the freedom to focus intensively on ballet and their prospective career. Pressures also tend to be less overwhelming in the handling of frequent exams, projects, and homework assignments. For some, school work may become more enjoyable, since lessons can be tailored to a student's specific needs, interests, creativity, and learning pace. Naturally not all programs are equal, and some provide a much more varied, in-depth, and challenging syllabus than others.

Convenient as scheduling flexibility may be, there is also something to be said for the value of the traditional school structure, which teaches one to handle academic pressures and accountability and encourages socializing with peers unaffiliated with ballet. Home-schooled students dedicated to ballet may miss out sadly on these important social interactions. Unfortunately, there are only so many hours in one day. The friendships and connections with nondancers that I formed during school hours certainly kept my life in balance and helped keep me from becoming obsessively consumed with ballet; a "bun-head," if you will. I became aware of just how special studying ballet was, and how unique it made me. I truly came to appreciate the many choices and sacrifices I had made and would continue to make in the name of my career.

Another benefit of middle and high school, I found, was the exposure to a variety of teachers who had specialized in the individual subjects they were teaching. Several of them remain constants in my mind. They sparked in me new interests, curiosities, and talents that I might not otherwise have thought to pursue or develop; writing is one of them.

Full-time arts academies, where the curriculum includes both academic classes and rigorous ballet training within one functional environment, are a practical and beneficial option. Many such academies in the United States are tuition-free public schools, while private arts schools usually offer scholarship programs for those who qualify. Many also provide boarding and housing options for out of town students. The High School Program of University of North Carolina School of the Arts (UNCSA) is one of the most reputable such academies in the country. Douglas Gawriljuk, former full-time faculty member and director of summer intensives, believes that there are great benefits to be found at these types of schools. Young dancers are provided the advanced opportunity to collaborate with other students immersed in varying artistic avenues of study, such as drama, music, visual arts, design, and production; fields that dancers will surely encounter later on in their careers. Another benefit, according to Gawriljuk, is that "students are able to study both dance and academics together, and parents can feel safe knowing that their child is living in a completely safe environment." He advises that students be willing to commit to a rigorous schedule before choosing a school like UNCSA, because "the typical daily schedule can be very intense. A high school student's day at UNCSA will start out at around eight o'clock in the morning, go until approximately six in the evening, and consist of several different dance, arts, and academic classes. Those involved in productions will then attend additional rehearsals from seven fifteen to nine thirty at night. It is definitely a full-time commitment!"

Where there is a will there is a way, and any schooling option can eventually lead to a successful career. There is no right or wrong option set in stone. The key is figuring out which environment will allow one to work most productively, finding an individual balance between dance and academia, and mapping out one's own individual path to success.

Tips

∾ When choosing a ballet school, at any level, investigate the teachers' method, dance style, and background. *Did they ever perform professionally? If so, when and where? How long have they been teaching? What have their students gone on to accomplish?*

∾ Watch a class or two to see if you identify with their approach. *What is the typical teacher:student ratio? Do they frequently have guest teachers come in? If so, how often? At what level are students allowed to participate in such classes? Do professional dancers ever come to do lecture-demonstrations or perform with the students during the year?*

∾ Make sure that the studios are large enough to accommodate comfortably the number of students enrolled in each class. Each studio should have full-length mirrors and—most important for reasons of physical safety—should be equipped with a sprung floor.

⊗ Last, do remember that training at a small school or company does not mean that your chances for becoming a professional will be any less, nor will training with a large, prominent school or company guarantee you automatic professional success. The ideal environment for dancers to train, and to dance professionally, is one where they feel happy, fulfilled, and able to improve steadily. We are human beings above all else, each with different individual needs and desires. Listen and follow *your* own instincts to lead you to the right avenue for you.

The Dreaded Decision

College or Career?

The time will surely come in all young ballet dancers' lives when they are faced with the colossal responsibility to make a huge, life-altering decision. Should they follow their peers off to college or take the risky plunge into auditioning and possibly dancing professionally? They will confront a giant fork in the road and wonder which path is the right one to follow.

Without a doubt, some will have trouble seeing eye to eye with their parents concerning these issues. I can still feel a bottomless, nauseating pit in my stomach as I think back to the moment when I stood before my own parents and boldly declared that I had decided to postpone my college education in hopes of pursuing my career. I swallowed my fear down in one gulp, hard as a lump of coal, and braced myself. I was positive that such an assertion would surely arouse the argument of the century. My mind had been set for a long time. I had unwaveringly convinced myself that if I went off

FIGURE 2. Baby ballerina
(in my beloved pink tutu and tiara).

to college with my friends, I'd be obliged to abandon my lifelong hopes and dreams. It was not that I didn't want to further my education, but I knew that a traditional college schedule would never allow me time to dance in a company. If I let four long years pass before auditioning, I thought I'd never find a position in a reputable ballet company. I'd be too old and inexperienced to compete with the younger girls striving for the same position. Heading off to college after graduation was simply a non-negotiable issue as far as I was concerned.

Fortunately, my parents did finally allow me a "temporary academic hiatus," during which I could take my chances on finding my way to a career in ballet. I was both thrilled and terrifically frightened. I was literally begging to be pushed out of the nest, unsure if I could even fly. In my case that big leap of faith turned out to be a blessing. I graduated and received my high school diploma, with honors, in the spring of 1993 at age sixteen. That fall I began my training full-time at the School of American Ballet, and I gained exposure to realistic competition, new teachers, company directors, and company auditions. The following spring (1994), I seized the opportunity to join Miami City Ballet as an apprentice. Eighteen years later, I'm still with MCB, where I have been a principal dancer since 2001.

In hindsight, I was presumptuously naïve to think that the choice between college and career had to be strictly black or white. For one reason or another I had developed an "all or nothing" mentality, when in fact there are several tried and true options for dancers who wish to continue to higher academic learning. For dancers who are not certain that they want to pursue ballet exclusively, or for those who would like to expand their horizons, arts colleges and universities can provide exposure to a broad range of different styles and techniques. For those who may be lacking fluency in alternative dance styles, this exposure helps develop versatility and also leads to a wider range of prospective job openings down the road. Many universities offer their dancers the chance to test out other dance-related avenues; areas of study that may prove helpful in embarking on a second career—for example, teaching, psychology, nutrition and health, physical therapy, anatomy, dance criticism or journalism, and even photography.

Dancers interested in higher learning should not feel that shouldering a four-year (full-time) college curriculum is the only way to go. Presently there are several options allowing for dancers to seek out and maintain a dance career while earning a college degree. Many universities now offer "set your own schedule" online programs and classes, while others offer evening or early morning classes tailored to working students who prefer to learn in a classroom setting. Some colleges even offer credit for life experience and performing experience. There are also several universities that have begun working in conjunction with major ballet companies and a program called Career Transitions for Dancers to provide dancers a higher-level education. Lessons may take place online, in classrooms, or on company grounds.

Ashley Knox and Tricia Albertson, longtime dancers with Miami City Ballet, have both decided to delve into a college education while continuing to dance full-time. Feeling a bit consumed by ballet, Knox was looking to create a better balance in her life. "I wanted to learn new things, use my mind in a different way, and discover new interests. Being exposed to people outside of our dance world 'bubble' has shown me that there are other possibilities in life, and at the same time has given me a deeper appreciation for being a dancer," she notes. "I will take only one academic class at a time during the season. That way, I can stay focused on my dancing and find enough time to do my schoolwork well." Albertson yearned to occupy her mind in a different way as well and was surprised to discover that college would become another outlet for her to excel and feel proud of her achievements. She loves learning new things and applying herself in new ways. Taking online classes exclusively for the last several years (comfortably, at her own pace), she is now only a few classes away from earning her degree. "As wonderful as dancing is, it's not a career that will last forever," says Albertson. "We will all have to reinvent ourselves and choose a second career at some point. Change leads to growth in a person, and you never know where life may lead you. Having a solid education can open all kinds of doors and can help you see life through a different lens. You may even discover a new interest that engages you just as deeply as dance does!"

As I reluctantly tiptoe toward the inevitable end of my own dancing career, a day that once seemed very far away, not a moment goes by when I don't wish that I had some college credits under my belt. As I wonder what my next career step will be, I think: *Wouldn't it be nice to have a degree in business or arts management to help me in running my own company or school one day? Wouldn't it have helped me to have taken formal courses in writing to help me pen more books in the future? Wouldn't it have served me well to have studied early childhood development or psychology if I want to work with children in dance one day?* The list could go on and on.

On the bright side, I wholeheartedly dedicated all of myself, completely, to my career. In that regard I have no regrets—only great achievements. My mind is eased knowing that it is never too late to learn. On the other hand, it's never too early either. "I'd advise young dancers to take one class at a time," says Knox. "Chip away at it slowly while dancing your heart out. Keep learning and stay curious! Being a well-rounded person will only help you to be more successful in ballet, and in life as a whole."

3

Gracefully Handling Scrutiny

The Art of Successful Auditioning

The first and scariest audition I ever took was for acceptance into the summer program at the School of American Ballet. Most kids join the program from out of town and attend large open call auditions in their own cities. Being from New York, I was offered a semi-private audition with the famous Antonia Tumkovsky ("Tumy," as she was known by her students). Three other girls and one boy and I felt very small in the most gigantic studio I'd ever seen. Entering the room followed by the pianist, the school's director, and the registrar, Tumy was a frail little thing; an elderly lady with a tiny white bun and bangs, big friendly blue eyes, and the sweetest looking red lips. She walked with a cane, one of her legs dragging along in a limp.

Upon first impression, I wasn't the least bit intimidated until . . . *whap!* She hit the floor with the cane and demanded sternly, "Do me first position. *Pliés!*" (a bending of the knees, usually the first exercise of the ballet *barre* warm-up; see glossary). Instantaneously she became a fierce drill sergeant, and my stomach began to crawl up into my throat. She came around to each of us and tested our flexibility, range of turn-out, and feet and then intimately scrutinized our preteen physiques; up, down, and all around. During the process she was making several comments in Russian to the school's director Madame Gleboff, who would then have the registrar make notes in her book. Every so often Ala, a voluptuous Russian pianist, would let out a chuckle or a grunt.

In what seemed like an eternity (but was actually under an hour), the audition was over. Just like that, she turned back into the sweet little old lady who had first entered the studio, gave us all a little smile, and left. I ran out to my teacher, who was waiting in the hall, and she exclaimed, "Good girl! You did it, you're in!" Though I was excited to have done well, I was in such shock over what I had just experienced that I was not sure how to react.

Years later I would find myself in an entirely different scenario. An open audition for Miami City Ballet was being held at the School of American Ballet studios, and it seemed as if every dancer in New York was in attendance. Edward Villella had been watching classes all week at the school, and a friend of mine was just dying to try out for a place in the company. I hesitantly complied, feeling responsible to offer her moral support, but I had no real expectations of my own. I figured it would be a learning experience, at the very least. With a number pinned to my chest, I wedged myself into an open sliver of space at the barre. After every few combinations, groups of dancers were eliminated. Each time a number was called out, I was sure mine was next. The class continued, and I gradually started gaining confidence. This class was fun! It was quick, jazzy, and very unusual for a ballet class. It was intriguingly different from the classes I was used to attending. The combinations really invited me to *dance*; I was moving better and faster than I ever thought I could, and I began to smile. I made it through to the center—*adagio* (slow movements concentrating on control), *pirouettes* (controlled turns on one leg), and then jumps. I was having a blast, but it seemed too good to be true. Any minute someone was bound to realize that I was very weak and technically in way over my head. The class was wrapping up, with only about fifteen of us left; it was time for *fouetté* (whip) turns. My heart sank. This was sure to be the end of me. I gave it my all, my best shot. Not quite managing sixteen turns, I stopped and smiled, nervously trying to hide my embarrassment. I backed up hesitantly, as inconspicuously as I could, toward the back of the room as the other girls continued. They did doubles, triples; I knew I couldn't compete with that.

The audition ended, and Mr. Villella thanked us all and assured us he'd be in touch. Truthfully, I never thought I'd hear from him or Miami City Ballet ever again. *How could they have kept me in that studio as long as they had, comparing me with dancers who were much stronger, much more capable than I?* It must have been an oversight on their part. It made no sense to me. About two months later, when I had just about managed put the whole experience behind me, I was notified by the school reception desk that MCB was on the other line … I had a job!

Auditioning may feel quite natural for some, but it can be downright agonizing for others. No matter how one feels, it happens to be an uncomfortable, ongoing reality of a dancer's life. Even employed dancers are expected to audition on occasion to be cast in specific roles or ballets. Some may also have to audition to be promoted, as is customary in the Paris Opera Ballet. A choreographer who is unfamiliar with a company may hold an "audition" to assess each dancer's capability or to decide who may be best suited to the choreographer's movement ideals. It is best to accept and become comfortable with auditioning; as a dancer one will not soon escape it! The more auditions one attends, the more familiar the routine becomes. Measures can be taken and preparation skills can be developed that may end up giving you an advantage over the rest of the crowd.

Keep in mind that most directors are looking for clean, long lines, so be sure to arrive suitably dressed. Wear a neatly pulled together outfit that accentuates your best features, discreetly camouflaging any flaws. It is best not to cover up at all, but skirts are generally accepted for the ladies. Sporting a short one in lieu of a long one will help to accentuate the legs without hiding too much. One should choose a leotard that complements the figure (sleeved leotards tend to balance out and visually slim the appearance of wider hips better than do camisole styles). Do keep outfits simple; for ladies a leotard (wearing a solid, brightly colored leotard may help dancers stand out in a crowd), pink footed tights worn underneath the leotard, and *pointe* shoes if called for. For the gentlemen, a simple leotard or form-fitting plain-colored tee shirt tucked into footed tights, or secured in a knot behind the back, is customarily the best option for classical auditions. As a rule dancers should not wear anything baggy. Unitards have also become an acceptable and popular alternative for both genders.

Hair should be neatly pulled back away from the face, and for ladies, tightly secured into a bun or twist. Hair flying around will end up being a distraction to both the dancer and the spectator. The same holds true for bulky jewelry and accessories. Leave big watches, bracelets, necklaces, and dangly earrings at home. Come to the audition as simply as you possibly can.

Nerves and butterflies in the stomach can very well be a good thing, but they can also make a dancer feel ill! It is important to remember to eat and be properly energized to sustain yourself and perform at your best throughout the audition. Stick to eating the same healthy way you normally do. Your body is in no need of any extra surprises. Do come prepared with healthy snacks to keep you going throughout the day, since some auditions can last for hours. Also drink lots of water (bring your own bottle) to ensure that you stay well hydrated.

Executing combinations in the first group can positively paint a portrait of confidence. Pay close attention to what is being asked for musically, choreographically, and stylistically. Directors always appreciate versatility in a dancer and the willingness to adapt.

Dancers are usually expected to arrive at an audition prepared with a well-formatted, up-to-date resume of training and professional experience (if any), and two recent 8 × 10 photos: one headshot and one dancing shot (the most common is a simple "First arabesque" position in a leotard and tights). A brief note or cover letter describing one's interest in training at that school or in dancing for that particular company is also a nice touch.

Above all else, stay calm, cool, and collected. Remember, there is a fine line between proactively exuding self-confidence and sacrificing one's humility. Mentally approaching the audition as if it were a performance may help dancers stay in the right frame of mind. Dancers should be themselves, believe in themselves, and focus on *themselves*. It is a waste of time and energy to get caught up in what others are doing or what the director is presumably thinking, whispering, or writing down. An auditioning dancer only needs to concentrate on being the best dancer that he or she can be. Directors want to see personality shine through someone's dancing; they look for and appreciate individuality.

In professional auditioning, the last step is usually going out on one's own to take a class with the company at their studios or at a theater if they are on tour in a city near you. When directors see a dancer again, outside the typical "cattle-call" audition atmosphere, they can more easily focus attention on that dancer specifically. Auditions like these are normally held on an invitation-only basis. In these instances a dancer will need to call, write a letter or e-mail, and usually submit a DVD before being invited.

Tips

✎ Arrive early and give yourself ample time to warm up before the audition begins. The barre work during an audition class is usually judged just as much as the center work, and dancers may be cut before the barre is even over. If you are warm beforehand, you will be able to show off your full technique from the get-go. Being warm will also help to protect you from strain, as the class may be structured differently from what your body is used to doing.

✎ Do keep in mind that directors often hold auditions in search of a specific type. If you aren't chosen, try not to get discouraged! The decision is not personal and does not necessarily reflect on you or your capabilities; you may in fact have exactly what someone else is looking for. Finding your place in the right school or company is sometimes a trial and error process leading to a fundamental partnership between dancer and director. As dancers we can't always understand what reasoning lies behind the decisions that a director makes. Take each audition in stride, and use each one as a learning experience for the next.

4

Going for Gold

Ballet Competitions

Freezing cold air poured out of the vents of the tiny art house cinema, and I fidgeted, trying to wrap myself cozily into my sweater. The lights began to dim as I settled down into my seat. I was brimming with curiosity about the film I was about to see: *First Position*, a documentary directed by Bess Kargman, produced by Rose Caiola. Six aspiring ballet dancers, ranging in age, are followed from the start of their intense preparations through final performances and judging of the famed Youth America Grand Prix—currently one of largest and most prestigious ballet competitions. There was a buzz of busy-bee chatter coming from a group of pre-teen dance students a few rows behind me. I smiled inside, detecting their excitement, and hoped for them that the film would hold true to both the marvels and the harsh realities these competitions comprise. There can be so many rewarding benefits but also innumerable disadvantages connected to the world of competing in dance.

When I was growing up, my teacher never really proposed to her students the idea of competing formally. It seemed that for her, ballet was strictly a performance art, not a competitive sport. To be sure, the nature of the dance world at that time was different. Generally speaking little emphasis was placed on ballet competitions, and the prestigious ones that did exist were few and far between. Nowadays, competing has become commonplace, and many students believe that if they don't participate and compete, they will find themselves at a disadvantage when the time comes to secure a job. As far as my experience has demonstrated, however, there is no need to worry. There are many professional ballet dancers, including myself, who continue to make fantastic careers for themselves and have never participated in a formal competition.

What competitions don't guarantee, however, is success. Young dancers should understand that if the idea of competing seems unattractive, several other roads can lead to scholarships and careers. The notion of formally competing at anything has always made my stomach turn. Though I absolutely love to perform, I can't stand the thought of being technically scrutinized and judged for a score. When I turned sixteen, my teacher surprisingly suggested that I enroll in the Prix de Lausanne competition in Switzerland. She warned that I should have no expectations—this would be just for "the experience." I dutifully agreed, but truthfully the very idea of being in that scenario scared me to death. The trip turned out to be costly, and given the level of my dancing at the time, chances are I would not have made it very far in the competition. Ultimately we decided against it. Relief! I could breathe again. Looking back, I know that had I in fact made it there, my insecurities would surely have gotten the better of me. Nevertheless, my destiny was scripted. The following year I leisurely attended one of the many open auditions being held at SAB; just for the experience, with no expectations. It was for a young Balanchine-based company then on the rise called the Miami City Ballet. The rest is history.

Students, teachers, and parents should discuss together whether competing is a challenge that a young dancer is ready for and willing to tackle. Competing does provide a great forum to exhibit technical strength, and it allows students the chance to size themselves up against other students in the same age range from around the world. It is a great way to get a realistic idea of where one stands and how much, how quickly, and in what areas one may need to improve.

If a dancer is confident of being able to perform at a high level, then competing can be a fantastic way to get noticed by the dance world at large. It also provides one with objective feedback from some new sets of eyes. Dancers who compete well may even come home with a medal—the standard gold, silver, or bronze. Additional acknowledgment prizes are also awarded, such as for the strongest overall performance or best in any given age group. Major school and company directors are often judging or in attendance, and separate scholarships (and even apprentice/trainee positions) are awarded to exceptional competitors, offering a wide-open door to the beginnings of a career.

As always, along with all of the positives come downsides that one must be sure of being equipped to handle. Being judged can trigger intense feelings of pressure and stress. One must put oneself in a professional's state of mind, which is easier said than done. Criticism can be harsh, and though it is not meant as a personal attack, it can still be painful. To stand their ground, competitors need to give more than 100 percent and be ready to handle major disappointment. It may turn out that even the best of efforts are simply not enough. Surprises may also present themselves; competitions are notorious for having slippery performance and rehearsal floors, and dancers usually have little time to get acclimated to the performance space. The size of the stage may be very different than in the space where one has rehearsed, and adjusting quickly to the lighting and wing space may prove challenging. One must arrive mentally prepared to focus internally, adapt quickly to a new environment, accept criticism, and tune out distractions to be truly free to perform at one's best.

Tip

❧ If you do decide to compete, make sure to have all solo variations and *pas de deux* (steps for two) you plan to perform extremely well rehearsed. Selections should accentuate your best qualities and also establish your versatility. Do be cautious of over-rehearsing. Try not to focus on one small series of steps from a solo or on specific tricks to only one side. Doing so can ultimately be detrimental; it can create imbalances in technique and development and can also lead to injury. At the end of your preparatory period, a piece should feel comfortable, well prepared, and finely tuned but still fresh and exciting.

5

Ballet Is Ballet, Right?

Getting Acquainted with Different Styles

One of the attributes I have most enjoyed at Miami City Ballet is its strong rooting in the Balanchine style. Many people, even some frequent ballet-goers, don't really understand what this means, and for a time I wasn't exactly sure myself. As a student, I just loved watching different ballet videos at home and with my teacher. At the studio we'd usually watch the classics, such as *The Sleeping Beauty* and *Swan Lake*, but there were others as well. She called these "Balanchine ballets." At the time, the main difference I noticed was a lack of story line, which I later realized does not apply to all Balanchine works. Eventually I came to understand that Balanchine was not just the name of the choreographic genius, but it had become a term used to describe an entire technique—a specific way of dancing ballet. Without my realizing it, my teacher had been exposing us to this, and other techniques, little by little.

There was a time when ballet companies were branded for specializing in a particular style. The New York City Ballet focused on Balanchine, American Ballet Theater danced the classics, the Kirov also danced classical ballets but in its own Vaganova style, and the Joffrey Ballet danced primarily contemporary works. Today companies all over the world are softening their boundaries and incorporating several different styles into their repertoires, creating artistic diversity. For dancers, certain styles will always feel more adaptable and organic than others. To be truly valuable to today's directors, though, one must be versatile enough to dance them all.

My own versatility has grown tremendously over the years. I have performed all sorts of stylistically diverse ballets, such as *Agon* (George Balanchine), *Nine Sinatra Songs* (a Twyla Tharp ballet danced in high heels), *Afternoon of a Faun* (Jerome Robbins), *Piazzola Caldera* (a modern tango-based Paul Taylor work), and *In the Upper Room* (another Tharp work that I dance in running shoes). Sometimes I'll dance a combination of three of these different styles all in the same evening. Though my training was classically based from the start, frequent exposure to different techniques at a young age has definitely been to my advantage.

A strong base in pure, unaffected, classical technique is the key, as my teacher Teresa Aubel believed. This is the foundation that a dancer always falls back on, and it later allows for easy adaptation to several different styles. Several schools have adapted the Vaganova method of training. This typically "Russian" style fuses together elements of traditional French technique from the romantic era with the athleticism and virtuosity of the Italian school. The Vaganova method is complex and aims to produce a clean and virtuoso technique.

In the intermediate to advanced years of training, dancers should undoubtedly familiarize themselves with the Balanchine style. Balanchine classes focus on developing long, exaggerated lines and large movements as well as building meticulous footwork, speed, and musicality (this is later translated into Balanchine choreography—known for its distinct musicality, precision, and attack and danced by almost every company today). I have found that my work in the Balanchine technique has also helped me to pick up the contemporary and modern choreography that we sometimes dance. It has made my movement quality more malleable, less rigid, and has helped me become more versatile and coordinated in general.

During my high school years I was exposed to the Martha Graham modern dance technique. Though the structure was not entirely dissimilar to that of ballet, I must admit it was not my cup of tea. I am grateful for having had some experience in it, though. It has helped me to understand the grounded, weighted, "breathier" movements from the core that I've encountered in Paul Taylor and Twyla Tharp works.

Whichever technique a dancer is based in, a general understanding of several others will prove useful when joining a company. I believe that a dancer's duty is to try to dance any given style as authentically as possible, and the easiest way one can accomplish that is through knowledge.

Tip

❧ The more styles you can familiarize yourself with in the latter years of training, the better off you'll be when seeking a dancing job. These days most directors and choreographers look for and value a dancer's versatility, which distinguishes individuals as "useable" or "moldable." If your school focuses on only one type of training, then try to explore supplemental classes at open studios, summer intensive programs, or workshops to gain exposure to different styles, but never discard or disregard your hard-earned technical foundation and background.

The Dancer's Uniform

Adapting to a Dress Code

I anxiously anticipated attending my first ballet class in the pink tutu and tiara that my grandmother had given me for my birthday. Just gazing at it would give me lovely butterflies in my stomach. Believe me, I loved that tutu so much that I would have jumped at the chance to eat, drink, and sleep in it had I been allowed! To my dismay (and protest), on my first day of class I learned that tutus were *not* permitted as classroom attire. They were "costumes"; only worn onstage for performances. Girls were expected to wear leotards to class. This new realization definitely put a damper on things, but I quickly resolved to settle for the second best option: a prized article of clothing—my one and only leotard, in strikingly bright cherry red nylon, with perfectly cropped cap sleeves.

Was I in for a giant shock! When I stepped into my very first ballet class, I looked around the studio and realized that something was not quite right. I was a bright red bull's-eye in a sea of black. I had been excited to arrive dressed in my favorite color; but how quickly my feelings changed. I hated standing out from everyone else and my face began to flush, almost as red as my leotard.

The teacher quickly informed my mother that there was indeed a dress code, and I would be expected to adhere to it, just like the other girls. My mother agreed, but she wouldn't have time to buy me a black leotard that week. I'd just have to manage in my red one. The following week came and went, and there I was, still standing out like a throbbing sore thumb. "Please!" I begged "I just *have* to have a black one!" Just when I started getting used to the shame, I did indeed get my very own black leotard. What a relief! I was finally able to blend in. No more embarrassing ruby for me. But with age people change; a few years down the line I'd give *anything* to be allowed to wear a different color and stand out from the crowd.

Like most students, I was obliged to wear the customary uniform of black leotard and pink tights for just about every single year of my ballet training. I soon came to despise that color combination and loathe pink tights in general. In my early professional years I refused to wear them unless I was onstage and had absolutely no choice. My resentment over the uniform eventually withered away. Some days I actually prefer wearing pink tights since they allow muscle definition to be seen more clearly in the mirror. Though I won't often wear a black leo/pink tights combination in the studio, stage attire is another matter. Ironically, the black and pink ensemble is staple costume for several Balanchine ballets. Like it or not, I can't escape it.

Teaching has helped me appreciate and understand the benefits of a dress code. It enables teachers to correct a dancer's body easily, and it instills a certain discipline in students. During summer intensives, schools are usually more relaxed in their rules, allowing students to wear colorful leotards of their own choice. Pink full-footed tights (without runs or holes) remain a requirement, however, and skirts are usually only allowed for pointe and variations class. Instead of their usual uniform (white tee shirt or leotard), boys are free to wear any color tee during summers, as long as it is knotted or tucked into black tights. For both boys and girls, neatness is always mandatory, and jewelry is almost always forbidden (other than small stud earrings for the ladies).

Professionals are generally permitted to wear whatever they like for class and rehearsal. While I am appreciative of this privilege, I am still mindful of my choices. I always try to wear neat, well-fitting dancewear pieces that coordinate somewhat in color. I love wearing earrings, but I never choose anything too large, dangly, or distracting for dancing; and I *never* wear hoop earrings unless they are specifically called for as part of a costume. They can be dangerous to dance in; if someone's finger were to get caught, an earlobe could easily be torn.

Though I do like to wear legwarmers and heavy knits in class to help me warm up more quickly, I try to make myself remove them for rehearsals. If my feet and knees are covered up, hidden from sight, I tend to get lazy about stretching them completely. If I can see them clearly in the mirror, and

I know that the ballet mistress can see them too, laziness is not an option.

Dancers should remember that just as in any other profession, our appearance sends out a message about what kind of artists we are and can determine whether or not we are taken seriously. If a lawyer entered a courtroom for a trial wearing brightly colored workout gear instead of a formal suit and tie, he would not come across as a self-respecting professional. It is the same in dance. If a dancer comes to an audition, a class, or a rehearsal wearing overly baggy warm-ups, has messy hair, is wearing huge earrings or other jewels, or has large, noticeable holes in the day's clothes, chances are that dancer will not be seen as a serious self-respecting professional either.

In the outside world it is politically incorrect to be judged on one's looks, but in our world, dancers are asked to "put on appearances" all the time. It is part of our training, and part of our job. Adhering to it shows directors, teachers, ballet mistresses, and fellow dancers that one truly respects and cares about the work and the environment. I personally tend to dance better when I'm happy with how I look. If I'm not comfortable with the outfit I'm wearing, it becomes a chore to look at myself in the mirror all day long. Every evening I carefully choose what I'm going to wear the next day according to my rehearsal schedule. I plan out what I think I'll feel most comfortable in, depending on the ballets I'll be dancing. For example, if I know I'll be partnered a lot, then I'll choose a leotard made with nonslip fabric, and I'll make sure that it fits well in the right places so that I don't have to keep adjusting it. It is a bit of a process, but when I feel good about how I look, I can concentrate better on my dancing. Since we spend more time in our dance clothes than our street clothes, it makes perfect sense to select outfits carefully that make us look and feel great.

Tip

& Old tights can be cut up, turned upside down, and made into tops that can be worn under or over a leotard for added support and warmth. Cutting out the crotch makes an opening for your head, while cutting off the feet allows hands to pass through when your arms are inserted into the legs of the tights. These homemade tops are an ideal addition to any dancer's wardrobe. They are very form fitting, won't interfere with partnering, don't hide as much of the upper body as typical sweaters do, and—best of all—since they're recycled, they are very economical; always a plus for students and dancers on a budget.

It's a Love-Hate Relationship

A Ballerina and Her Pointe Shoes

A faint odor was beginning to consume the air, stinging the noses of all the girls in the School of American Ballet residence hall. It grew more pungent as the minutes passed. As we investigated the halls, we were met with a film of smoke emerging from the cracks under the kitchen door.

"Someone's shoes are in the oven!" one student shouted. "They're burning!" cried another. As dancers ran down the hall, mouths and noses covered, the fire alarm began to blare. I stood still, paralyzed. My jaw dropped and my stomach sank. There really was a pair of pointe shoes on fire—and they were *mine*!

One might wonder what my shoes were doing in the oven in the first place. Well, that was one of the many strategies that I attempted in hope of rehardening my old, worn-down shoes. Creative as it may have been, I can't take sole credit for my ingenious plan. I was assured by one of my classmates that if I applied wood varnish to the tips and soles of my shoes and baked them in the oven at 350 degrees for twenty minutes, they would come out as good as new—but one important detail was missing. I should have *preheated* the oven and then turned it off before placing my shoes inside. Luckily my naïveté did not burn down the residence hall, but the stench did linger for a few days. My souvenir of the event was a charred black pair of shoes that had once been a lovely delicate pink, and they were hardened all right; to a crisp! Not ideal for dancing, to say the least.

Pointe shoes are the single most important piece of equipment that a ballet dancer uses. In the right pair we can feel liberated; steps freely flowing out of the body without the least bit of struggle. In the wrong pair we can suffer—from achingly painful and bloody toes to missteps and falling down or serious foot and ankle strain or injury. Finding the right pair of shoes brings to mind Cinderella and her glass slipper. It is an ongoing trial and error process, which can end up being downright frustrating. A dancer should be patient and avoid settling on a shoe that is merely adequate; a pointe shoe should feel exactly right. Trust me; it will be worth the exhaustive search. Unsuitable shoes may create struggles for a dancer when one is rolling through the feet or finding one's center of balance. Ideally, we should never feel as if we are struggling with or battling against our shoes.

There are many elements to consider in choosing the proper shoe for each step of the development process, but the unwavering factor that will forever remain most significant is proper fit. Not only will a form-fitting shoe feel and look best on the foot; it will also help prevent injuries. The

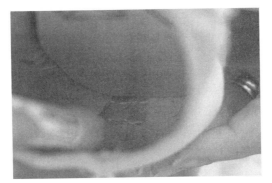

FIGURE 3. Hardening the inside tips.
Shoe photos © Leigh Esty Photos.

box and shank will likely break down in the right areas, and the shoes will be more supportive and last longer in general.

Sadly, pointe shoes are a great expense, and not every parent or young dancer can easily afford to replace them on an ongoing basis. Averaging between sixty and eighty dollars per pair, they quickly become an extremely costly necessity. Advanced, professional grade shoes are often priced at the higher end of the spectrum and, ironically, tend to have the shortest lifespan when it comes to durability. When I was studying, my shoes would last for about a month. (Little did I know that when I became a professional my shoes would last for just one or two performances!) Knowing how extremely costly they were, I tried my very best to make them more durable. Under my teacher's supervision, I hardened them with all kinds of concoctions; I tried spray shellac, wood varnish, and floor wax. I even took them to the local shoemaker to have him add leather insoles.

Now that I am a professional, MCB provides me with the shoes I need each season, at no cost to me. I receive an allotment of around eight pairs per month. While this may seem like an abundant supply, it really is not in view of how much I actually rehearse and perform. I always need to reinforce them before I even put them on my feet, just to make them last through the month. All it takes for me to harden them sufficiently is a tube of superglue or a few drops of Jet™ glue poured into each tip. Another product that works well is Hot Stuff® by Satellite City Glues. It takes a bit longer to dry than superglue, but the extra wait time is worth it. Hot Stuff works wonders for hardening the insides of the shanks, the box and tip, and also the outer sole. Several professional dancers I know use it religiously. All these glues have proven to be cost-effective and time-efficient ways to get the task done. The best one for the job depends on the individual.

There are two types of shoes mainly available today. Shoes made with traditional paste are usually hand made using natural materials, while those of the more modern variety are machine made using synthetic materials. While the latter are likely to be more durable and consistent, the former tend to conform more easily to the shape of the foot as they break in. Strength and level of support is always determined by the construction of the upper box and the shank insole. Dancers should try out both types of shoes to decide which is best for them.

I now wear custom-made shoes, crafted to my specifications, but this was not always the case, and for those not yet in a professional company this is rarely an option. Stock shoes can serve just as well, but I cannot stress enough the importance of being properly fitted for each pair of pointe shoes by an experienced salesperson and, if possible, under the supervision of one's teacher. Feet tend to change size and shape throughout one's studies, so an exact fit must be ensured every time a new pair of shoes is purchased. Take note that every brand and style of shoe fits differently and offers varying degrees of support. Several different pairs should be tested to find the right one. It is important to have a stock shoe brand and size in which one feels truly comfortable dancing before one joins a company. Special orders often take a long time to arrive for new company dancers, and it may be an ongoing trial an error process to figure out the specifications that are appropriate (apprentices and trainees are often not even granted the luxury of special-order shoes). Adequate stock shoes will be provided for several rehearsals and performances in the meantime, so be sure to know which ones work best.

Most dancers "break in" or soften their shoes before wearing them in the studio. I personally like to step on the box (the front vamp area) of each shoe to flatten them out, and bend the shank (the hard support insole) back and forth a bit at the ¾ point to soften it up. Some dancers prefer to flatten the box and soften the shank by wedging the shoes into a door jamb and moving the door back and forth. It may sound silly, but there are many who do it. Most shoe companies advise not softening the box at all before wearing the shoe. Doing so improperly can diminish the strength of the shoe and inhibit its ability to provide proper support.

FIGURE 4.
Elastic placement and stitching.

FIGURE 5.
Ribbon placement and stitching.

Honestly, I have never been able to wear them straight out of the bag, and I don't know of any dancer who has. A little bit of break-in prior to wearing helps the shoes form more easily to the feet and just makes them more comfortable.

The proper positioning of the ribbons and elastics before sewing is also crucial. I'm often asked by nondancers why pointe shoes don't come with the ribbons already attached. Ribbons are not purely decorative. Their true job is supporting the foot and ankle. Each foot needs customized support, and improperly placed ribbons and elastics put the foot in jeopardy. When sewn at specific angles and distances from the seams of the shoe, ribbons help hug the shoe to the instep and create a much prettier line of the foot. The way a dancer sews the ribbons is an individually developed art.

Sewing my shoes is tedious and time-consuming, but it has become important to me. When I traveled to Paris for coaching in the title role of *Giselle,* I met the gorgeous French ballerina Elizabeth Platel, then an *étoile* (starring dancer) with the Paris Opera Ballet. She took one look at my shoes and threw them back at me in joking disgust. It seemed that she had never seen such a sloppy sewing job. I did not understand what the big deal was; after all, no one can see the stitches from a distance. She calmly explained her point, which I'll never forget. *"You must take pride in your shoes, your feet, and yourself, chérie. If you don't, and can't even bother to sew your shoes properly, why should anyone bother or care enough to watch you dance?"* I was humiliated; speechless. She was right, no contest, but no one had ever put it so bluntly.

Sensing my embarrassment, she shared with me one of her own personal tricks. She revealed to me that she tied the knot of the ribbons on the outside of the ankle, as opposed to the inside (as most dancers do). This made the line of her foot in *tendu effacé* (stretching of the leg and foot at an oblique angle) look much more beautiful. It was crystal clear that she paid attention to even the tiniest detail.

As a performer, I've learned the importance of sewing my shoes securely. A ribbon popping off a shoe during a show is unacceptable, unprofessional, and dangerous. I always sew with heavy duty or crochet thread; both are much stronger than regular thread. Some dancers use dental floss for

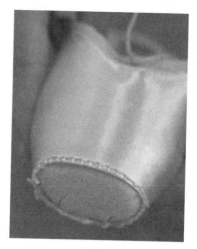

FIGURE 6. Darned tips.

its durability, but I have always found the stitches tend to slip out after just a few rehearsals. I stitch securely around the perimeter of each ribbon and elastic edge, being careful not to catch the drawstring. For performances, I'll sew the knot and ends of the ribbons to my tights after tucking them in. This keeps them from coming loose and from moving around while I dance. There is nothing more distracting than a dancer's ribbons dangling from her feet! Clear Band-Aids® can be used to keep ribbons and knots tucked in if time is an issue, and a little dab of rosin will work to hold ribbons in place during rehearsals or class. Ribbons should *never ever* be secured with safety pins; doing so is extremely dangerous!

Shoes should not be worn unless proper time is taken to sew on ribbons and elastics correctly and securely.

Most students dream anxiously about the day when they will slip on their first pair of pointe shoes. As glamorous as it seems, it is not something to be taken lightly. It is a serious advancement, and teachers have a responsibility to make sure that their students are physically strong enough and technically capable of graduating to pointe work. There is not a specific age when a "pointe alarm" goes off; the decision to begin pointe work should be made based on a student's progress rather than age. Being put *en pointe* too soon (usually before age eleven) can result in injury, since the bones of the foot are still in the developmental hardening stages. Waiting too long is not beneficial either, however. After the age of fourteen, the feet may become less pliable and lose some of their potential for flexibility. It is a tough call to make, and there are several factors that can influence a teacher's decision. Dancers need to be patient. Pointe work is a hard-earned reward, and the better prepared dancers are from the start, the more they'll end up enjoying it!

Tips

❧ If you do not move on to pointe work at the same time as your friends, don't worry. Everyone is unique and develops at a different pace. Speak with your teachers—perhaps there are some exercises (such as Thera-Band® work) that can help you develop the extra foot and ankle strength needed—or try to find a pre-pointe training class that will help build muscle awareness and alignment specific to pointe work.

❧ If you are not a fan of shiny satin, or the ballet you're dancing calls for your shoes to be "pancaked" or matte, blotting the satin with pancake foundation makeup or using a paper towel to dust the shoes with a bit of rosin works wonders. It provides uniformity between the tights and the shoe, visually lengthening the line of the leg. If you are trying to match a dark complexion, bare legs, or flesh-colored tights, then spraying the shoes with an appropriately colored shoe spray (found at local shoe repair shops) is usually the best bet. You may need to experiment and layer a couple of colors together, as I do, to arrive at the perfect match for your skin tone.

❧ If shoes feel a bit too snug at first around the box, where they bend for *demi-pointe* (half toe), try blotting them with some rubbing alcohol. This will help soften them up without overly breaking down the glue. Avoid using water on the box, which can destroy the paste and warp the shoes.

☙ Since so much emphasis is placed on beautiful lines of the legs and feet in ballet, some pros have started cosmetically enhancing their arches, though doing so is still relatively controversial. There are different arch pads available for purchase, or they can be made using light padding and first aid tape. When worn in the proper place underneath tights, they can significantly improve the look of an underdeveloped arch. Be careful though—if they are not fitted correctly, or if they shift around while you are dancing, they can have just the opposite effect and look ridiculous, so use them at your own risk!

☙ Remember: hang onto some worn shoes even if you've moved on to a new pair. Certain ballets will require the use of softer shoes—helpful for jumping, fluid foot work, and choreography requiring off-balance pointe work. It is best to have a variety of different shoes available, in different strengths and levels of the break-in process, ready to go at all times.

See how I sew on my ribbons and darn the tips of my pointe shoes here:

https://www.youtube.com/watch?v=s0zFjBfYGiI

8

Treat Your Feet

Banishing Corns, Bunions, and Blisters

I slipped on my first pair of pointe shoes as a young girl of about twelve years old. Finally! I had them! The rush of excitement was a wonderful anesthetic and I just wouldn't take those shoes off. I *bourréed* (moving the feet on pointe in very small quick steps) around in them for hours, without protection, until each one of my toes was swollen, blistered, and bleeding. I looked down proudly at my new "real ballerina" feet. When I tried to put on my street shoes to go home, a pain shot through me like I had never felt before. I was so traumatized that from then on I exaggerated my toe care tactics to an extreme.

Looking back, I have to laugh. I would begin by covering each toe with a plastic bandage and wrapping each profusely with first aid tape. I'd follow this with a coating of lamb's wool and top each foot off a protective toe-pad. I went to such an extreme that it soon became difficult to squeeze my "protected" foot into my shoe. This would eventually cause me new problems—painful bunions and corns in between my toes. Not only was all of this precaution silly and unnecessary—it actually hindered my dancing; I could no longer feel the floor.

After the three or four years it took me to wean myself off this ritual, by padding each toe the tiniest bit less each week, I began to realize that not every toe was a target for pain. I forced myself to take a few classes free of any padding at all (only slightly torturous) to pinpoint where exactly my shoes were rubbing the most. I found that *my* particular problem areas are the tips of my first and second toes and the side of my little toes.

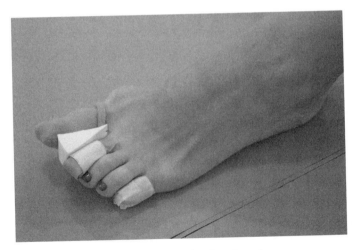

FIGURE 7. Feet protected and ready to dance.
Photo © Leigh Esty Photos.

My toe care routine has become very simple—a protective gel toe cap (I use Bunheads® Jelly Tips™ by Capezio) placed over each big toe, a plastic bandage placed vertically over the tips of my second toes and secured with a little tape, and my pinky toes wrapped with paper tape or masking tape. I don't need to use any other traditional padding in my shoes at all.

All dancers have their own ways of tending to their feet. Female dancers are in pointe shoes for an average of six hours per day and must take measures to stay as pain-free as possible. Male dancers also experience a lot of toe pain, believe it or not. For example, my husband, Carlos Guerra, a longtime principal dancer with MCB, has performed with the pain of a big toe toenail that had cracked completely in half, and I know of others who have danced with infected and ingrown toenails. But no matter how much men may endure, most can't imagine what it feels like to have to dance directly *on* their toes all day.

Some of my fellow dancers go to great lengths in protecting their feet; some use abundant amounts of 2nd Skin® Moist Burn Pads, others wrap their feet in paper towels, and some cut up socks to place inside the tips of their shoes. Each dancer is unique, and only experience will help you determine your ideal path to less pain. When I danced at the Kennedy Center in Washington, D.C., for the *Balanchine Celebration* (on the same bill as the Bolshoi and American Ballet Theater), I noted that star ballerina Nina Ananiashvili would take her shoes off backstage between her major entrances in George Balanchine's *Mozartianna*. I watched her in disbelief;

should I do that, my feet would swell terribly. I would never be able to get my shoes back on in time to make it back out onstage. It seemed to work wonders for her though. She was magnificent.

The two most important things to try to avoid when using any type of protection are losing the feeling of contact with the floor through the shoes, and severely altering the fit of the shoes to compensate for the padding. For shoes to be properly sized, all padding that will be used should be brought to a fitting and worn while trying on shoes. Since feet change in size and shape over time, dancers must remember to reevaluate their sizing and protection needs every now and then.

Though toe pain can sometimes be maddening, professionals cannot take their shoes off at every small hint of discomfort. Ballet dancers need to build up resistance, including some calluses, to be able to withstand pain and pressure on the toes. Professionals are expected to keep their shoes on throughout the whole day (which can last up to seven hours), and one needs to build up to this gradually. To build tough feet, shoes should be worn for as long as possible each day, sometimes during off hours. Some dancers wear their shoes while washing dishes and around the house when starting off the season with softened feet, helping them to rebuild their resistance. Applying Compound Tincture of Benzoin or CTB (likely available at your local pharmacy) to delicate, sensitive skin on the toes is one way to ward off blisters. Often used by athletes, it has a reputation of toughening and hardening skin through repeated exposure. (*Note:* CTB should be used only on clean, unblistered, healthy feet. If any redness, pain, or itching occurs, stop use and see a doctor immediately.)

Should the occasional blister erupt, a warm Epsom salt bath can be soothing. Disinfect with Neosporin, and be sure to keep blistered skin as clean as possible by washing with soap and water. Keeping it covered with a moist burn pad, or a bandage designed specifically for blisters, will also provide some extra relief. If repeated blistering occurs, ill-fitting shoes may be to blame. Shoes that are too narrow or too wide can put unnecessary pressure on certain areas, causing friction and blistering. Since feet often change size and shape, a refitting and evaluation may be the simplest solution.

Corns, a different matter entirely, need to be addressed in their own way. Corns are patches of toughened skin, formed in the shape of a cone, with the tip pointing downward into the foot. Their growth is encouraged when sweaty toes are trapped in tight shoes for long periods of time. These little guys are common and can be extremely painful. Hard corns usually erupt on the outside of the toe and sometimes need to be shaved down in order to heal properly. (*Note:* Shaving should *only* be handled by a professional podiatrist. Attempting to shave a corn oneself could lead to further irritation and infection). A soak in a warm foot bath with baking soda will help to soften skin, as will wrapping a cotton pad saturated with vinegar on the affected area. Once the dead skin is softened, it can be sloughed off with a pumice stone. Slathering on a paste of aspirin mixed with lemon juice will also soften skin and provide relief. Tying a small piece of fresh pineapple or pineapple peel to the area overnight is said to work wonders, though I have never tried this trick myself. The natural enzymes and acid that pineapple contains may reputedly even *cure* a corn rather quickly. Salicylic acid remedies bought over the counter eventually dissolve a corn with repeated use. The acid breaks down the proteins that make up the hard corn and softens the upper layer of dead skin. I try to avoid these remedies myself, since some of them can be quite irritating. (*Note:* Do proceed with caution; *never* use salicylic acid on open or broken skin). If all else fails, a good old-fashioned ice pack will stop pain from a hard corn right in its tracks and provide immediate relief.

Soft corns are different and tend to erupt under the skin in between the toes. These types of corns should be kept extremely dry to promote healing. After sweating, showering, or swimming, feet should be dried well with a towel and then dried additionally in between the toes with a hair drier set on "cool." Cornstarch powder can then be applied to absorb any moisture that may build up inside a dancer's shoes. Cushioned corn pads and moleskin are great for relieving pain and pressure; however, keeping feet dry, using thin foam or gel spacers in between the toes, and wearing properly fitted shoes will help prevent corns from forming in the first place.

Bunion growth is also common in dancers, and severe bunion pain plagues many, both male and female. Bunions are a result of the inward lateral deviation of the big toe, and as the bunion develops, the tissues surrounding the joint can become red, swollen, and painful. Wearing shoes that are wide enough in the box and long enough in the vamp to accommodate sensitive areas will help to alleviate and avoid extra pain and pressure. I have found that bunion cushions make my shoes feel tighter and aggravate my pain, but others enjoy relief when using them. Toe spacers, whether store bought or homemade (triangular makeup wedges will do the trick), can help to keep the big toe joint in alignment and alleviate pain as well. Keeping the big toe joint aligned from the beginning of one's training can help to discourage bunion development in those who are not already predisposed to this condition through heredity. Big toe alignment can be reinforced outside one's pointe shoes. Often this is done at night by wearing a small brace, which can be ordered through most medical or physical therapy websites. Similar results can also be achieved through professional taping.

Tips

✇ Prevention is the key. Spend the time it takes to tape up and protect sensitive areas *prior* to dancing to avoid any abrasions and discomfort. Do not use any more padding than is really necessary. The goal is to prevent pain and problems, not to create new pressures.

✇ If a corn or bruised toenail has got you cringing and you need a quick fix to numb the pain, using Anbesol® (or any over the counter oral anesthetic gel) is a known trick of the pros. Though conventionally used to numb teeth and gums, it can work the same magic on toes and toenails. Apply to the affected area and rub in well. Let it dry and repeat. Make sure it is completely dry before covering with tape or bandage.

(*Caution: Do not use Anbesol or any similar product on open blisters or broken skin.* Doing so can lead to major infection. If an open blister remains raw, won't heal, or seems to be infected, seek out the help of a podiatrist or medical professional immediately before the situation becomes more serious and sidelining.)

❧ Practice healthy hygiene! Washing feet with mild soap (be sure to dry well) in between classes and rehearsals, and washing toe pads regularly, will help prevent fungus growth under the nails and in between the toes. If your feet are emitting an unusually strong odor that does not subside with regular washing, a fungal infection may be the culprit; seek immediate treatment from a doctor or podiatrist.

Find out how MCB principal dancers Jeanette and Patricia Delgado keep their toes safe and protected here:

https://www.youtube.com/watch?v=-xLtaqb9BDM

9

Looks for Your Locks

Mastering Ballet Hairstyles

In school I was always under the impression that a bun was a bun. Sure, they could be pinned up high or low, but basically how much could a *chignon* (bun) really change? I was taken completely by surprise during my first tour with MCB. I was required to wear a high Balanchine-style bun for my first ballet of the evening, a French twist (specifically rolled bottom to top) for the second, and a romantic low bun for the third. I was responsible for making all this magic happen within the fifteen-minute intermission allotted between pieces. I also had to change costume, tights, shoes, and headpieces. Impossible! I tore into my hair in front of my dressing mirror like a maniac. Fumbling and making a mess, I glanced at the other dancers, who seemed to be calm and collected, effortlessly pinning up their own tresses. Not only was I uncertain of what the specific differences were between the styles; I had no notion of how to arrange and secure my long thick hair in any way but one. I did know one thing—this was not the moment to stop and ask questions. Haphazardly I brushed, combed, pinned, and sprayed my mane into what ended up looking like a rat's nest. My only consolation was that this was just a dress rehearsal. I had the rest of the evening and the following day to practice and try to perfect my hair styling techniques.

Fifteen years later I have tremendously improved and developed my hair styling tactics. Whenever we dance a ballet calling for a specific style, I can now serve as an example; a model to follow. Getting to this position was not effortless. I practiced and experimented until I perfected what I like to call the basic ballet styles, and I try to continue expanding my style repertoire with each new piece that I dance.

As a principal dancer I am allowed much more leeway than before in choosing my hairdos for any given ballet, and I always try to create one that is characteristic of and adds an element to the role I am dancing. For example, when I danced the role of Caroline in *The Lilac Garden*, I tried to create a Victorian-inspired up-do by loosely pinning several sections of hair on the top of my head. When I danced the role of Ava (a 1940s Hollywood screen star) in Edward Villella's "Foxtrot: Dancing in the Dark," I rolled my hair under and back, stuffing foam rollers inside for additional height.

The first and probably most significant bun I had to learn to make for myself was a Balanchine high-style bun. This chignon differs from any other high bun in that it truly lies directly on the crown of the head, not in the middle. Originally, back in the 1950s and 1960s, it was a lot smaller and a bit perkier; a topknot of sorts. It has since evolved, and these days it is flatter and slightly elongated, which creates a beautiful shape of the head in profile and visibly enhances and elongates the neck.

For me this style is most easily achieved by starting out with a neatly pulled back high ponytail, tightly secured at the crown of the head. I divide my gathered hair in half (top and bottom), and twist the top half tightly. I then start to pin it down little by little (inserting large, strong open hairpins or roller pins at forty-five degree angles) in a jelly roll shape, forming it into a bun of its own. I repeat the same steps with the bottom half of my ponytail. When complete, the top and bottom buns together resemble a figure eight. Last, I wrap both halves together in a hairnet, secure the bun with a few

The Balanchine high-style bun (figs. 8–13) lies directly on the crown of the head. Photos © Leigh Esty Photos.

FIGURE 8. First gather and secure hair at the crown.

FIGURE 9. Divide in half and twist around.

FIGURE 10. Secure top half of
bun with hairpins.

FIGURE 11. Repeat with
bottom half.

FIGURE 12.
Secure with hairnet.

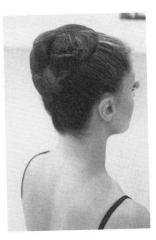

FIGURE 13.
Finished high bun.

more pins for good measure, and spray it generously with hairspray. (*Note: Always* use hairspray or some other strong hair fixative for performance. Frizzy and stray hairs are magnified tremendously under stage lights!)

The low bun is a simple version of the traditional *chignon*. Hair is gathered in a low ponytail and can be divided in

FIGURE 14.
Gather and secure hair in a low ponytail.

The low bun (figs. 14–16) is simpler.

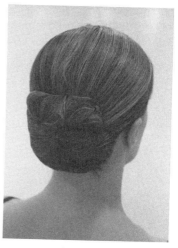

FIGURE 16.
Finished low bun.

FIGURE 15.
Secure bun with hairpins.

several different ways before being pinned down, or it can simply be coiled around the elastic band with no division at all. Low buns can have a part down the center of the head, or side of the head (my personal preference), and can easily be done with the hair pulled straight back, unparted, as well.

The French twist is a rather simple style, but it can be difficult to perfect for those with thick hair like mine. It usually takes a bit of practice to master this style. I start out by pulling my hair straight back into a low ponytail at the nape of my neck. I then begin to twist it to the right, which is easier for me, and pull the twisted pony upward. As I do this, I fasten the twisted part tightly to my head with strong open hairpins, not bobby pins. The loose ends of the ponytail can then be tucked under, for short-haired girls, or rolled into a bunlike shape at the top of the head, for those with long hair. Always spray this style *very* well, and tighten it with extra pins as needed. I like to shake my head hard, and spot my head around (as if I were doing a pirouette) when I'm done, to make sure that the twist is securely fastened to my head.

A softer, more romantic presentation is the Giselle style. This style will prove useful for several romantic, nineteenth-century classical ballets. It looks very old-fashioned, but it does lend itself well to the time period of such works. Perfecting this hairstyle certainly takes a little patience and extra repetition.

Practice makes perfect, so dancers should try out hairstyles at home prior to the performance to get properly acquainted with each new style. In effect, this is yet another rehearsal to add to one's typical daily routine.

The French Twist (figs. 17–21) can take a bit of practice.

FIGURE 17.
Gather hair in a low
ponytail.

FIGURE 18.
Twist and lift
upward.

FIGURE 19. Continue
twisting and wrap
ends under.

FIGURE 20.
French Twist top view.

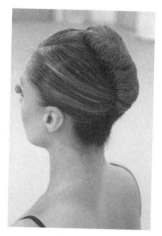

FIGURE 21.
Finished French Twist.

The Giselle style (figs. 22–25) is more romantic.

FIGURE 22. Gather and secure a low ponytail, leaving front hair out.

FIGURE 23. Fold back front pieces and secure with bobby pins.

FIGURE 24. Make normal low bun in the back.

FIGURE 25. Finished Giselle style.

Tips

✄ Believe it or not, slightly dirty hair works best for most styles. If hair has been freshly washed, it tends to be slippery and hard to secure. During performance weekends try not to shampoo too often—just rinse thoroughly or use a dry shampoo to get rid of product residues.

✄ If you have stubborn or curly hair at the nape of your neck that won't stay put with hairspray alone, try brushing it upward first with clear mascara. The tiny brush bristles easily grab and coat each hair, allowing the hairspray to adhere better. Clear mascara is great for taming unruly eyebrows too!

✄ To prevent hair breakage, a common problem among dancers (we weaken hair by constantly pulling it back so tightly), give strands a break on your days off. Wear hair loose and avoid using heavy products. Save the slick look for performances. On class days, opt often for more softly pulled back tresses and alternate styles. Wet hair may be easier to secure, but it is also more susceptible to damage. Dry your hair well before putting it up to avoid unnecessary stress on strands and scalp.

Watch me demonstrate how I create the ballet hairstyles described:

https://www.youtube.com/watch?v=RmYe_-IlP1w

10

Fancy Face

Stage Makeup 101

Each time that I perform, particularly in character roles, I take some time to think about how to enhance my transformation into each specific character, mood, or persona through my makeup. For example, when I dance the role of the Sugarplum Fairy in *The Nutcracker* I always apply a little glitter dust to my cheeks, arms, and upper chest. The sparkles catch the stage lights and create a magically radiant glow. One day while I was practicing some last minute steps before the curtain went up on act two, I noticed one of the little "angels" staring up at me in amazement. I glanced over at her with a smile, and she asked, "Miss Sugarplum, are you really made of magic? Look, you're sparkling!" I told her it was fairy dust that was making me sparkle so brightly. Her eyes widened with wonder. From then on I have not danced a single show as the Sugarplum Fairy without my glitter. It is a special touch that adds a little magic, for me, for the children dancing with me, and I hope for the audience as well.

Before makeup can be enhanced with special touches, one must be very well practiced in the basics. There is a general technique for stage makeup application that is the foundation for almost any ballet or role one will have to perform. Step one is having a makeup kit well stocked with the correct supplies:

1. Pancake makeup (both your skin tone and white)
2. A porous sponge for base application
3. Loose powder—translucent or skin tone
4. Black "wispy" false eyelashes and glue (for ladies only)
5. Powdered bronzer for contouring
6. Rosy pink powder or cream blush (*Note:* Boys use a more neutral peach or beige)
7. Eye shadow (black, brown, blue, white, beige, peach)
8. Waterproof liquid eyeliner (black, brown)
9. Waterproof eyeliner pencil (black, white, brown)
10. Lipstick and lip liner (red and dark pink for girls, brown for boys)
11. Eyebrow pencil (dark brown) and brush

High-quality makeup brushes varying in size and shape ensure easier makeup application. As with painting, specific brushes aid certain strokes. Brushes should be washed regularly and kept clean. A soiled brush will deposit color where it is not wanted, and color will not deposit evenly if there is excess sebum or oils on its fibers. The easiest and least expensive method for keeping brushes clean is soaking them

FIGURE 26. My makeup kit. Photos © Leigh Esty Photos.

for about thirty minutes in a bath of baby shampoo and water. Be sure to rinse them thoroughly and let them air dry completely.

Dancers develop their own specialized makeup routines over the years. We are usually expected to make ourselves up on our own, without any help, except for the occasional opinion from fellow dancers. Discovering which techniques work best is an ongoing process. Makeup needs to be adjusted to suit different skin tones, eye shapes, and bone structures, but the most basic application steps will usually suit everyone:

≈ Starting out with clean moisturized skin, dampen the applicator sponge and swirl it around in the your skin tone pancake foundation. Using gentle strokes and blotting motions, apply it evenly all over the face, neck, shoulders, and upper chest; application to the arms and back is optional for most dances. For a "white" ballet (a ballet primarily danced in white tutus with dim lighting, in which the ballerinas are typically ghosts, swans, or sylphs, such as *Swan Lake* or *Giselle*), the same method applies, using white pancake in place of the skin tone. Avoid getting too much sun close to your performance dates, since the combination of sunburned skin under white makeup can give your complexion a purplish hue under the blue-toned stage lights, even with darker skin.

❧ Once the foundation has completely dried, the next step is to shade the cheek bones, temples, and jaw line with the bronzer. This accentuates bone structure and when seen from a distance creates a well-defined, contoured face. Next, a generous amount of blush (for the girls) should be applied

FIGURE 27. Apply contour bronzer below cheek bones.

FIGURE 28. Contour nose with brown shadow.

FIGURE 29. Apply glue
sparingly to false lashes.

FIGURE 30.
Apply to lash line.

to the "apples" of the cheeks and around the hairline for light-haired people. Boys should use a darker color, and a lighter hand.

~ Next come the eyes. I like to apply my false eyelashes first (boys skip this step). I feel this gives me a better shape and canvas for the rest of my eye makeup. I apply a small amount of glue to the eyelash strip and blow on it a little to make it tacky. Then, looking down into a magnifying mirror, I gently press on the lashes as close to my natural lash line as possible. Finish with a little mascara.

~ Once confident that the glue has dried and lashes are secure, start applying a beige, peach, or light blue eye shadow to the eyelid up to the crease. The crease itself should be shaded with a darker color (black, brown, or blue for girls, brown or black for boys). White shadow can then be used to highlight the area just underneath the eyebrows; the brow bone.

FIGURE 31. Liquid liner, eyelid.

FIGURE 32. Liquid liner, bottom lash line.

FIGURE 33.
Finished closed eye.

FIGURE 34.
Finished open eyes.

FIGURE 35. Lip liner.

FIGURE 36. Lipstick.

❧ Next comes the trickiest part—eyeliner. With a very steady hand, line the upper lids close to the lash line with a slightly thicker than normal stroke. This line should extend out a little past your natural lash line, making the eye appear larger. The bottom line is essentially applied in the same fashion, just a little farther down from your own lash line. The white liner can then be used to line the inner rims of the eye, as well as to highlight the inner and outer corners. This technique helps to prevent you from looking cross-eyed from a distance.

❧ Using your eyebrow pencil, the brows can now be lightly shaded in and extended outward just a touch (be careful; they should not extend out farther than your lashes).

❧ Next is outlining the lips with lip liner and filling them in with a matching lipstick. Blotting them well with a tissue and dusting them lightly with loose powder will help the color to last longer.

❧ Dust your whole face lightly with the same loose powder, or lightly mist with a setting spray, and you'll be ready to hit the stage!

Tips

❧ Be sure to cleanse your face thoroughly after every show. The heavy oils and pigments in stage makeup, along with sweat, tend to build up and stay clogged in pores, causing breakouts. If your skin is especially sensitive, look for hypoallergenic makeup, creams, removers, and cleansers.

❧ Avoid sharing eye makeup products with others. The eyes are sensitive, delicate, and prone to contracting infections spread easily through liners and mascara. Help your eyes stay healthy by keeping your eye makeup products off-limits to others.

My step by step stage makeup application demonstration:

https://www.youtube.com/watch?v=W-boaK6H-h8

11

You Mean Dancers Actually Eat?

Understanding the Importance of a Healthy Diet

Without fail, at every post-performance party I've attended, dancers gather around the buffet table piling food upon their plates, and one of the guests invariably remarks, "Wow, I didn't know that you gals actually eat! I mean, don't you need to watch your figures?" Or, "Are you really allowed to eat all that?" In response to this frustrating stereotype, I smile and say, "Well, of course. We do have to watch our figures, but yes, we do eat—often a *lot*! Imagine exercising for six hours or more every day like we do; wouldn't you get hungry?"

Contrary to popular belief, even the slimmest of ballerinas must eat several healthful meals and snacks throughout the day to remain strong and energetic. In fact, we rely on them. Our slender physiques are the result of our healthful food selections and rigorous regime of daily exercise. We absolutely cannot starve ourselves. Choosing the right foods to eat, and the right times to eat them, may even boost metabolism. I understand that from the audience's perspective, most of us look like delicate waifs who scarcely weigh more than a feather; but the truth is that we all have very different body types. Some dancers are long and lean; others are more compact and muscular. The one characteristic we all share is that we are not just artists; we are athletes. For some of us, weight management takes little or no effort at all. For others it presents more of a challenge. It is important to get to know one's own body so as to compose an eating plan that works best for maintaining an aesthetically acceptable yet healthy body. Please note that I call it an eating plan, not a diet plan.

The ballet world is brimming with negative body and self-esteem issues, especially among girls. Adolescent body changes can be a daunting adjustment for a ballet student to handle, and dealing with the remains of "baby fat" during your teenage years can be trying; it certainly was for me. These issues seem to be harder for dancers to handle than for average teens, perhaps because we are fixated on our reflections in the mirror all day long. We are obligated to dress in skin-tight attire and are constantly judged on our appearance. This can be taxing to one's self-image, especially during times of significant physical change. What young dancers should remember is that we must all learn to work as best we can with the body with which we were born. One thing is for certain—puberty does not last forever! Most often the extra pounds gained during these years are shed effortlessly later on, all by themselves. The biggest mistake dancers can make is to stop eating or go on crash and fad diets. Not only are these methods ultimately ineffective, but they can lead to lethargy, eating disorders, long-term weight gain, and even serious injuries.

As athletes, we need to provide our bodies with substantial nourishment consistently throughout the day. Food is the fuel that keeps our engines running. In our youth, during the important growth and development years, dancers' bodies need to receive adequate nutrition to keep working the way that we are demanding they do. Throughout adolescence especially, the body depends on calories to fuel the continuing growth of important bone mass—something we rely on to keep injuries like stress fractures at bay. Inadequate calorie intake does lead to weight loss, but at a very hefty price. Ryan Sobus, MPH, RD (a registered member of the Academy of Nutrition and Dietetics), warns that this kind of weight loss is generally a result of a loss of muscle and body fat.

Though most athletes concern themselves with loss of muscle, loss of body fat can have an equally sidelining effect. According to Sobus, our bodies require a certain amount of essential fat. In men, the minimum amount of essential fat is 3%, while in women it is 12%. Too little body fat can lead to chronic fatigue and susceptibility to illness in general. For women it can also inhibit the production of sex hormones such as estrogen—leading to the "female athlete triad," a syndrome that plagues several professional dancers and ballet students. This disorder includes three interrelated conditions:

1. Inadequate calorie consumption that has led to weight loss and too little body fat.

2. Amenorrhea—an absence of a menstrual cycle for at least three months.

3. Osteoporosis due to low estrogen levels (part of amenorrhea). Estrogen deficiency leads to bone resorbing and loss of bone mineral density, leaving bones more brittle and likely to experience a stress fracture.

In season, or during heavy training, females over eighteen years of age need to consume approximately 20–23 calories per pound of body weight, while males over eighteen need approximately 23–25 calories per pound. Sobus warns that these figures are generalized, representing the minimum requirement to *maintain* a healthy body fat level. If a dancer is already underweight, then restoration to a healthy body fat range may require an even higher caloric intake. The most accurate way to determine your own specific calorie needs is to have your resting metabolic rate (RMR) checked through a simple breathing test. This test takes about ten minutes to complete using indirect calorimetry (see glossary). Testing sites can be found at gyms, doctors' offices, or universities. Once one's RMR is determined, multiplying it by an activity factor of 1.5 produces an accurate calorie requirement figure.

For example:
Estimated RMR 1,600 × 1.5 = 2,400
Actual RMR using indirect calorimetry 1,850 × 1.5 = 2,775
Note: For the most accurate results, it is best to use a factor obtained through an actual RMR test rather than simply using an estimation. Below the age of eighteen years, the predicted number may be higher, since you are still growing and maturing.

Dancers should know that carbohydrates are an extremely important part of a healthy diet; red blood cells and the brain primarily use carbs as fuel. Red blood cells speed recovery and fuel performance since they carry oxygen to the body's tissues. Muscles also use carbs for their direct energy needs. Neglecting or eliminating carbs from your diet can lead to physical sluggishness and lack of mental clarity. In turn, your body may be forced to break down muscle tissue to produce its own energy. Sobus suggests that around 50–60 percent of one's total caloric intake should come from carbohydrates, but not all carbs are of equivalent nutritional value. Complex carbs, like those found in veggies, fruits, nuts or seeds, and grains will last with you throughout the day. Simple carbs, like those found in candy, soda, sugary juice drinks, and baked snacks will not. These may also cause a sudden rise and fall in blood sugar levels. After dancing, a starchy carb might serve you best, since that's when the body is most ready to reabsorb nutrients. Starchy carbs include potatoes, bread, pasta, rice, and certain veggies like corn. Whenever possible, try to make these choices of the whole grain, fiber-rich variety. Combining protein with carbs provides the most reliable source of long-lasting energy. (*Note:* The body can absorb a maximum of 2 grams of protein per kilogram of body weight, and protein should make up about 15–20 percent of your total calorie intake).

For sustained energy, efficient nutrient absorption, and muscle repair it is a better idea to eat several small meals and snacks throughout the day than the conventional three large meals. A healthy breakfast consisting of both protein (for building and replenishing lean muscle mass) and carbohydrates (for a fast-burning energy supply) is a *must*. A typical choice of mine is an egg white omelet made with some diced veggies and shredded low fat cheese, with a slice of whole wheat toast and half an orange. Another of my favorites is a half cup of plain low fat or nonfat Greek yogurt drizzled with honey, low fat–high protein granola, sliced raw almonds, half a banana, or blueberries and raspberries, accompanied by a glass of orange juice. It's almost like having dessert for breakfast!

After morning class I generally have a small snack to get me through the next few hours of rehearsal. A banana or apple with peanut butter, or a protein or fiber-rich whole grain granola bar usually keeps me going until lunch. I find that bananas and oranges are great for keeping potassium levels up during strenuous exercise, which reduces the risk of muscle cramps and spasms. Oranges also have a lot of fiber, which can help to keep me feeling satisfied until it's time for lunch. Grazing on raw nuts and dried fruit helps keep my sugar levels stable while also giving me a little extra boost.

At lunch time I usually enjoy a wrap, sandwich on whole grain bread, or salad made with fresh greens, tomato, chicken or turkey breast (for vegetarians, tofu or beans can be substituted), along with either a piece of fruit or carrot sticks with hummus. In the late afternoon I continue munching on other little snacks, such as trail mix, wheat crackers, baked snap peas, fresh fruit salad, or roasted soy nuts. I'll sometimes keep steel cut oats (made with skim, low fat, almond, or soy milk) dusted with brown sugar and cinnamon in the fridge, a cooler, or a thermally insulated lunch bag. It is a healthy, energy-sustaining snack, the taste of which reminds me of scrumptious rice pudding.

My favorite meal of the day is dinner and, of course, dessert. Like most male dancers, my husband (and fellow principal dancer), Carlos Miguel Guerra, is a huge eater. He normally insists on having a big dinner, and being Cuban, he loves his meat, rice and beans! Barbequing and Sunday morning breakfast aside, I have volunteered to be the designated cook in our household. I'll usually season and broil lean meat, chicken, or fish and accompany it with brown or jasmine rice, quinoa, or whole wheat couscous, a veggie (broccoli, asparagus, sweet potatoes, and corn are my favorites), and a salad with some diced avocado—a yummy healthy fat. (*Note:* Healthy fats are essential and help us to metabolize fat soluble vitamins like vitamins A, D, E, and K. A lack of vitamin D, especially, can lead to impaired bone health and a risk of developing stress fractures. Approximately 20–35 percent of your total caloric intake should come from healthy dietary fat). I normally leave the bean cooking to Carlos's grandma, Abuela, who prepares a different *potaje,* or homemade bean stew, for us almost every week. Yum! (*Note:* If you don't have your own Latin grandma on call to prepare frijoles for you, the canned variety does taste pretty good with a little added seasoning. Rinsing and draining canned beans well before adding them to a meal will remove some of the excess sodium that canned goods often contain. Making beans from scratch can take hours, but is also an option if you like to cook.)

Last but certainly not least, I never, ever skip dessert! It is a weakness of mine that I just have to satisfy. Besides, we work hard all day, so I believe that dancers earn themselves that small indulgence. I simply try to make intelligent dessert choices. My favorite sweet in the entire world is ice cream. In my own heaven, I think I'd be surrounded by quarts of Häagen Dazs and a giant spoon. I'd probably be as big as a house if I indulged in the full fat variety every day, though. Instead, as a "tutu friendly" option, I try to stick to low-fat ice cream, frozen yogurt, sorbet, or a portion-controlled novelty like an ice-cream sandwich or Popsicle. I try to keep my portion size between half and three quarters of a cup and top it with some fresh strawberries, banana slices, or chopped nuts. Sometimes I'll simply scoop it solo into a cake cup; there's nothing like enjoying a good old ice-cream cone.

If you need help making your own nutritional choices or creating a healthy eating plan with menus that are right for you (remembering that age, height, weight, gender, and frequency of physical activity are all important factors to consider), do consult with a registered dietitian, certified fitness professional, nurse, or doctor who can surely offer professional help and guidance. Bon appétit!

A Healthy Working Dancer's Sample Menu

Created by Ryan Sobus
(Based on a recommended intake of 2,500 calories/day)

BREAKFAST

¾ cup dry oatmeal

2 Tbsp. nut butter

½ cup Greek yogurt

SNACK

Banana and string cheese

LUNCH

2 oz. sliced deli meat

2 slices whole grain bread

½ an avocado, spinach, and tomato slices

10 Triscuit crackers

SNACK

1 cup cereal

1 cup low fat milk

1 cup blueberries

DINNER

5 oz. lean protein (chicken, beef, or fish)

2 cups rice, potato, or pasta

2 cups cooked veggies or large tossed salad

2 Tbsp. low fat dressing

DESSERT

150 calorie treat: ice-cream sandwich

Total calories = 2,500
Total fat = 69 g (25%)
Total Carbs = 365 g (57%)
Total Protein = 110 g (18%)

A Registered Dietitian's Advice

When the pressure to be thin outweighs your desire to be strong, what becomes the most compromised is your potential to dance for the long term. A professional dancer commits to hours of rehearsal and training daily, a job description that takes a tremendous toll on the body. If you want to go the distance in this field, you must take care of your bones. You can be lean, but associate "skinny" with brittle bones that won't stand up to the challenge, literally. This requires maintaining a healthy body fat percentage and fueling your body with the nutrients it needs for optimal performance.

—Ryan Sobus

Keep in mind that the more water you drink throughout the day to replenish fluids lost through sweat and exercise, the better you'll feel. If you don't like plain water, try flavoring it with fruit slices, cucumber slices, or a green tea bag. Please *stay well hydrated*, but do be careful of over-hydration as well. Both dehydration and over-hydration can lead to an electrolyte imbalance or hyponatremia, which may result in muscle cramping, nausea, dizziness, or even coma.

Sobus recommends determining the minimum amount of fluid you should consume daily by simply dividing your weight in half (I would calculate 110 lb. ÷ 2 = 55 oz or ~ 7 cups fluid per day). This may need to be adjusted depending on your water loss (sweat) and physical work load. The best way to determine hydration status is the color of your urine; a pale yellow or strawlike color means that you are hydrated, but anything darker means you are not. Every pound of water weight lost through sweat should be replenished through three cups of fluid.

Tips

There are a number of nutritional supplements that help in energy production and maintenance as well. Some of my favorites are:

◈ A daily multi-vitamin containing calcium, vitamin D, and fish oil.

◈ Emergen-C drink packets (contain vitamins C and B for sustained energy).

◈ Protein powders (either soy or whey—some of the boys in our company find these especially helpful for an extra boost).

◈ Low sugar electrolyte replacement drinks for quick rehydration on performance days.

◈ Glutamine (an amino acid that aids muscle repair), found at health food stores in powder or tablets. I like to add the powder to my smoothies. Glutamine promotes muscle recovery after intense activity, which in turn decreases soreness and fatigue.

❀ Pineapple, while being a wonderfully sweet and satisfying fruit, also has anti-inflammatory properties as a result of the bromelain enzyme it contains. It is a great fruit to enjoy at the end of a hard work day.

❀ Remember that energy bars and shakes, while great as occasional "on the go" supplements, should not be used as a replacement for real food at mealtimes. It is *extremely* important to try to consume a diet mainly consisting of whole foods that are minimally processed, making them more nutrient dense, and "live" foods, such as yogurt or the drink kefir, which contain enzymes that aid in the digestion process (these can be especially beneficial if you commonly experience gas and/or bloating). These foods have tremendous naturally occurring nutritional value, and their vitamins and nutrients are more easily absorbed into our systems than those artificially added into processed foods.

Note: Before beginning any eating plan, or adding supplements to your diet, be sure to consult a doctor or registered dietitian for healthy, optimal results based on your specific needs.

Step into my kitchen to see how I prepare one of my favorite healthful lunch choices:

https://www.youtube.com/watch?v=nLKjwP13Ei4

12

Keeping Your Instrument Well Tuned

Preventing and Handling Injury

It was my third class of the day at the end of a long week at the School of American Ballet. I was exhausted, but still I was trying my hardest to apply the many corrections that I'd been given earlier on that morning. Pirouettes were not my particular strength, and I desperately wanted to improve. I should not have pushed quite so hard, being as fatigued as I was; but I was stubborn and I did. Hindsight is always 20/20. I pushed off from my back foot, rose up onto pointe, tried to place my body correctly, spotted my head (the technique of focusing on a single spot while turning), turned, and somehow went around three times! Just as the excitement of completing a triple *pirouette en des hors* began to hit me, I landed in a position that was way over turned out and horribly misaligned—and I heard a loud *pop*.

For a split second time stood still. At first I had no idea what the noise could have been. But looking down at my leg, I realized in disbelief something was very wrong; my left kneecap seemed to be jammed off to one side. Without so much as a thought, I gave my leg a hard, swift whack, and managed to knock my patella back into place. I tried to take a step forward, and immediately my knee buckled. "No, no . . . *no!*" was all I could say. The room seemed silent and a million thoughts chased through my head. I suddenly realized that my leg felt very, very hot; then came the pain.

Hands glued to my knee, I faintly began to hear the drowned-out voices and commotion surrounding me, threatening to break my focus on the incredible sensations overtaking my leg. I tried to wish it all away as my heart started to race. I became nauseatingly aware of the excruciating throbbing that continued to get worse by the second. I felt my knee start swelling up under the tight grip of my hands, bigger and bigger. I tried as hard as I could to fight back the tears, but there was nothing left to do but cry. I was in my final years of training, and I was certain I had just ruined my chances for a professional career. In that moment I couldn't even imagine walking, let alone dancing. The teacher, Suzy Pilarre, managed to carry me over to a sofa in the lounge area where I could rest, and my friends rushed over with bags of ice. I was hurt, disappointed, and humiliated.

Eventually, that story had a happy ending. With a lot of patience and physical therapy, I did recover, and I did dance again; better than before, as a matter of fact. I hadn't ruined my chance at a career after all. I did learn a good hard lesson that day, though; our bodies are our instruments, and they are *fragile*. We use and abuse them every day, and there can be serious repercussions. If respected, maintained, and taken care of properly, they can perform miracles. If mistreated and taken for granted, they will undoubtedly break down on us.

Upon visiting doctors to have my knee examined, I found the consensus was that I'd better start thinking of a new career path. This would be a recurring injury that could eventually become much worse. I wouldn't hear of that! I refused to let their pessimism get the better of me. I remembered reading *I, Maya Plisetskaya*, in which the great prima ballerina discussed her own knee problems. Her issue was not so different from my own; she had a wearing down of the kneecap ligament, from her own body misalignment. She too visited doctors who practically guaranteed that, being cursed with chronic problem knees, she would never have a successful career as ballerina. In spite of them, and through hard work and perseverance, she managed a successful forty-seven-year career.

Her saving grace, and mine, was eventually finding a doctor who specialized in treating dancers and athletes. When workload, injury, and recovery goals are truly understood by doctors and therapists, and are met with determination and will by the patient, triumphant recovery is almost always possible. Reminders of the injury may linger (one may experience extra aches and pains on certain days), but they are usually manageable enough to dance through and overcome.

I had always been told that I was a lovely dancer but that I was "weak." Unsure what that meant exactly, I never paid it much attention. Why did a ballerina need to be so "strong" anyway? It was not as if I was going to go onstage and lift weights, right? Wrong! Every time we dance, we are actually

FIGURE 37. Pilates reformer. Photos © Leigh Esty Photos.

lifting and supporting a great deal of weight—our own body weight. The problem is that our ankles, feet, knees, and hips are delicate. They were not designed by nature to turn 180 degrees outward, nor to support our weight while standing upon our tiny toes. Since ballet constantly distorts our normal everyday alignment and balance, we need to make sure that all the muscles in our legs, feet, abdominals, and back are especially strong. They must work together actively to support and stabilize our bodies successfully in these unnatural *en pointe* (on toe) and *en des hors* (turned out) positions.

Some dancers are blessed with natural muscle tone and strength, but others, like me, need some extra help in developing it. Daily ballet classes may be challenging, but they alone are not always a sufficient method to build strength and

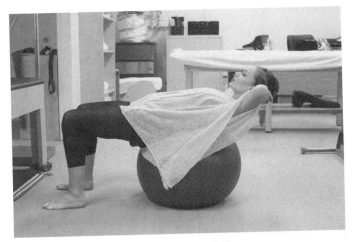

FIGURE 38. Physioball.

stamina. In this respect I found Pilates training, both mat and reformer exercises, very helpful in my later pre-professional years. It is extremely conducive to developing the long, lean muscle tone perfectly suited to a ballet dancer. As a professional I still enjoy Pilates, but I also practice yoga, have dabbled in gyrotonics, and have developed a special affinity for kettlebell work.

Gyrotonic® training, developed by Juliu Horvath with a dancer's physique in mind, is similar to Pilates in its focus on core strengthening but also addresses spinal mobility and pelvic mobility and stability. Training is mainly performed on an apparatus called the Gyrotonic® Pulley Tower. Exercises are designed to build simultaneously the strength and flexibility of the entire body through circular motions as well as to help develop an awareness of deep breathing. In gyrokinesis, also developed by Horvath, exercises are done seated on a specially designed chair and mat. They focus mainly on circular and spiral movements of the upper body, torso, and spine without bearing weight on the legs. Deep cleansing and warming breathing are specific focal points in this training system as well.

Kettlebell training is done with the use of light cannon-ball-shaped weights with a U-shaped handle resembling that of a tea kettle. They are swung, not lifted as traditional weights usually are, using momentum and drive from the trunk and legs. This swinging technique develops deep core stability and general coordination as well as shoulder girdle and leg strength. It also increases neuromuscular capabilities and partnering awareness. One must evaluate the kettlebell's weight, force, momentum, and pull (as one would evaluate these in a dance partner) and work with these, not against them. Medical exercise specialist and former dancer Michelle Khai describes kettlebell training as "an ideal modality to help prepare dancers for the reality of their performance context." "KB" training quickly became one of my favorites to practice. It has helped me improve both the power of my jumps and my cardiovascular endurance. "By using the whole body to manipulate the KB while moving through space, a dancer will learn to partner more easily, jump higher, and land safely," says Khai. "KB conditioning helps create lithe, lean bodies that move beautifully without undue muscle mass, critical to the dance aesthetic."

During the slower parts of our season, and especially on

our off-time, practicing a combination of several maintenance and training techniques helps me to work on using the weaker muscles that I don't typically feel in ballet, while giving my overworked muscles and joints a rest. I also benefit from increased stamina and endurance.

Practicing a cross-training regimen that works can help dancers stay in top shape and can help them remain injury free as well. Khai agrees that for intermediate to advanced dancers, class alone probably does not apply enough of a load to working muscles to build strength beyond what has already been achieved: "In fact, the body has a natural desire to become more efficient, so over time the neuromuscular system will fire fewer motor units within muscles to achieve the same tasks. Supplementing with a conditioning program throughout a dancer's training and career is actually a crucial step toward the prevention of injury and enhancing of performance."

It is crucial that dancers learn to listen to their own bodies. According to MCB's head physical therapist, Cynthia McGee Laportilla, MSPT, LMT, there are ways to differentiate normal, everyday aches and pains from dangerous and destructive ones. She indicates that after a hot bath, icing, massage, and adequate rest, general soreness usually subsides within one to three days. Injury pains, despite the same care, usually linger in the same defined area for longer. If a pain is sharp, stabbing, or throbbing, making it difficult to perform basic ballet movements (such as *plié or relevé*—bending the knees and rising onto toe or half toe) or even to walk, chances are an injury has been sustained. Also, when any area is unusually sensitive to the touch, heavily swollen, or discolored, an injury is most likely the culprit. In any of these cases Laportilla suggests that dancers seek the immediate attention of a dance medicine or sports medicine physical therapist or orthopedic physician, who will examine the problem and advise a dancer how to proceed properly. Dancers should elevate and ice the injured area five times per day and stop dancing until the injury can be properly diagnosed.

One of the most significant variables causing dancer injury is overwork or fatigue and lack of rest. Others include poor alignment and technique, poor physical conditioning, poor nutrition, dehydration, smoking, alcohol or drug abuse, stress, depression or anxiety, and negativity. Extracurricular cross training can help to decrease our odds of getting hurt but can never eradicate our risk entirely. Injuries, aches, and pains will always be a natural product of the ballet equation. Learning how to make the most of an injury will help keep you in a constructive and optimistic frame of mind if one does happen—a key component to effective healing.

My fellow MCB principal dancer Patricia Delgado has learned to cope with the emotional roller-coaster that being hurt can create. Having faced several career-suspending injuries over the years, she has learned how to find the silver lining within each experience. "It's heartbreaking to have worked your hardest to dance a role and then accept that, because of an injury, you just won't be able to. It's normal. You can't get angry at yourself. But you do need to allow yourself the right to feel sad," she says. Giving yourself permission to stop, recognize, and accept your feelings of disappointment is an important part of the healing process. "Sometimes, we just get so exhausted from our daily routine that we take dancing and performing for granted. We become complacent and sink into a slump. Being 'out' with an injury can really wake you up. It reminds you of how badly you wanted this career in the first place."

Though it is often hard to accept in the moment, things happen for a reason. Whatever the cause behind an injury, recuperation time can allow you the luxury to go back, erase, and rewrite certain not-so-satisfying things about your dancing if you let it. "We can really learn to use our bodies in a new, different, *healthier* way. Reworking your technique during and after healing will often help you come back to dance stronger, and even better than before," notes Delgado.

A chance to step across to the other side of the curtain, as Delgado often does, is another "perk" of injury downtime. "It is a gift to be able to watch your peers, dancers you admire, and the production as a whole. We need to be so internally focused when we dance that we don't always get the opportunity to benefit from the beauty and inspiration that surrounds us. When you're forced into the role of a spectator, you can really take the time to sit back and view everyone in a different and inspiring light. I've learned so much from doing that. I've grown as a dancer and an artist."

(*Note:* Cross-training, physical therapy, and maintenance techniques can't guarantee an injury-free career, but they can help you to undo and even prevent a lot of the wear and tear to which a dancer's body is subjected. Body awareness, care, and diligent maintenance can keep you dancing longer and keep your body healthier in general. Treat your body with tender loving care during your down time, and you'll feel the difference. Your dancing will be all the better, and your career all the more enjoyable.)

Tips

🕸 Don't be afraid to experiment with several different types of training to find the one with which you identify best. Go with a friend, and share feedback with each other. Whatever training you may decide to try, make sure that the instructor is aware that as a ballet dancer, you have specific needs. Trainers will alter their methods accordingly to suit you and will prevent you from doing anything that may be dangerous for a dancer's delicate frame.

🕸 *Be smart!* Ignoring painful and obvious symptoms of injury, and continuing to dance regardless without treatment, can eventually lead to further injury and complications down the line, such as chronically recurring and compensatory injuries. Recovery time may increase significantly and, in the worst case scenario, could shorten the length of your career. As hard as it may be at the time, try to think of the bigger picture. Your health and your career are worth whatever recovery time and treatment are necessary to heal your body properly. It took me a long time to accept this, but after several recurring ankle sprains, I have finally learned to be smart, listen to my body, and put things into perspective.

❧ Stretching can be a dancer's best friend, but only if it is done correctly and at the right intervals in your daily routine. A dancer's biggest mistake is habitually hanging out in a stagnant stretching position to "rest," "cool off," or just chat with friends. Worst of all, many of us do this first thing in the morning when we enter the studio before class. This can really do much more harm than good. It can cause repetitive daily micro-trauma to the soft tissues, a circumstance that can lead to injuries. It is best to leave deep, aggressive stretching for when your muscles are warm and will no longer be called upon to respond quickly, like at the end of a rehearsal day. Instead of warming up with a stretch, warm up instead with a rhythmic cardiovascular routine. This will raise heart rate and body temperature and help pump synovial fluid into your joints for lubrication.

❧ Remember to stretch out parts of the body that are normally overlooked, such as your iliotibial (I.T.) bands, which run along the outside of the thigh from the hip bone to below the knee (these tend to be tight and neglected on almost every dancer). Tight I.T. bands have caused me unnecessary knee and ankle pain in the past, so I have learned to stretch them out well. Seated on the ground, I perch my lower half sideways on top of a foam roller, sinking my body weight down into it, and roll up and down from hips to knees for a nice leg massage.

❧ Be cautious of exercising very frequently on the treadmill, bicycle, and stair machine. These tend to cause a lot of stress on the knees and other joints. Instead, try the elliptical machine, which provides a comparable cardio workout with far less negative impact. Practicing a floor barre (traditional ballet warmup exercises performed on the floor) is also great for building strength and enhancing technique. This method translates traditional ballet barre exercises into ones that can be done lying down on the floor, where the spine is fully supported.

✎ Work intelligently. Sometimes less is more. It's not about how *much* you do but about developing your craft in a conscious, intelligent manner. Give your body the time and nourishment it needs to repair itself and recover fully. Even if you don't feel tired, physiological fatigue from class, rehearsal, performance, and everyday life adds up quickly. Schedule in time to stretch, ice, self-massage, hydrate, nourish, and rest; when the time comes to perform, you'll be at your best.

✎ Try to recognize physical and mental fatigue, and don't work yourself to the point of exhaustion. Rest during breaks and get a *minimum* of eight hours of quality sleep per night (more during heavy rehearsal and performance periods).

✎ If you need to see a doctor for an injury, try to see one who specializes in dance medicine. This type of doctor has distinctive knowledge about the movements and skills required of dancers and the different variables that may have contributed to a problem or injury. If there are no such doctors in your area, Laportilla suggests seeing a board certified sports medicine orthopedist as the next best option.

Specifics of a Dance Conditioning Program

Created by Michelle Khai, BS, CSCS

1. Address imbalances: Dancers work so much in turn out that it is critical to try to restore joint balance by working in parallel as well. Also, if you know that one side of your body is stronger than the other, address this in your conditioning. The ballet tradition always has the dancer start with the right side. This develops an uneven skill set from left to right and also builds muscular imbalances, since one side is stronger than the other. Using a 2:1 ratio in the conditioning program can restore balance in the body.

2. Focus on deceleration: In addition to supporting movement from the core, focus on the deceleration aspect of strength training. Most injuries occur during the deceleration phase of a movement, meaning it is not the take-off for but the landing after a jump where injury usually occurs.

3. Periodized Conditioning Program: In order to avoid fatigue and burnout, balance out your dance workload with a supplemental conditioning load.

    a. *Off-Season*—where you will put in the most work and try to make your greatest physical gains in terms of strength, endurance, speed, agility, and flexibility. Train three times a week or more.

    b. *Pre-Season*—when dancers start back up with technique classes and a light rehearsal schedule. Taper off supplemental conditioning to once or twice a week, depending on overall workload.

c. *In-Season*—when dancers have a heavier workload with the addition of performances. Taper off to once a week, since the goal is now simply to maintain what has been gained in the off-season and pre-season work.

Take a sneak peek into principal dancer Tricia Albertson's PT session with MCB physical therapist Elizabeth Maples:

https://www.youtube.com/watch?v=LIhiQYuzffQ

13

Calling a "Time-Out!"

Dealing with Nerves, Stress, Anxiety, and Burnout

At the start of my career I had a wonderful friend who was not only a lovely dancer but also a beautiful person. In school she was adored by everyone, and her charm was like a ray of sunshine lighting up the room. Something about her changed after she joined a company though, and little by little she began to drift off into a very lonely place. She began excluding almost all her friends and family from her life and got so wrapped up her own mind and obsessions that she couldn't get out. She loved the ballet, but it was becoming an overwhelming chore, with which she never seemed to be satisfied. Stress weighed heavily upon her and she began crying all the time, both in the studio and out. One day she decided that she'd had enough and, sadly, just stopped dancing. If only she could have seen that she was not alone, her final choice might have been different.

Rest assured that we all have our moments of frustration, despair, desperation, exhaustion, anxiety, self-doubt, and stress. They are actually quite commonplace in an all-consuming and demanding art form like ballet. Several of the greatest dancers have struggled with frustrating stressors like nerves, for example, and have had to learn to conquer huge challenges like stage fright. As I apprehensively rehearsed for the unnerving opening solo of Balanchine's exceptionally challenging *Ballet Imperial* (a.k.a. *Tchaikovsky Piano Concerto No. 2*), famed dance critic and historian Robert Gottlieb assured me that before dancing the same role, the legendary Dame Margot Fonteyn would stand tensely in the wings thinking to herself: *If I can just make it through this first passage, then I'll be alright.*

The illustrious Allegra Kent suffered from performance anxiety as well. She has openly confessed in interviews and in her autobiography *Once a Dancer* that she experienced severe stage fright and even panic attacks before going onstage to perform. Who would imagine that a ballerina so beautiful often felt sick before stepping out onstage? I always thought once I became a principal dancer my pre-performance nerves would vanish, I would be satisfied with my performance more often, and the pressure of perfection and expectation would fade away. Ha! Not so. As a principal I put more pressure on myself than ever before, and I still get the "willies" (nerves, anxiety, and excitement) before every single show. We are our own fiercest critics. As the saying goes, it's hard getting to the top, but it's even harder staying there. It feels as if all eyes are constantly on a principal dancer to set an example.

Distressing as they may be, nerves can prevail only if one lets them. When handled well and channeled in a positive way, they can be a performance enhancer instead of an obstacle. The anxiousness I feel before a show is temporary and has even become somewhat comforting. If I don't feel an extra adrenaline boost from my nerves, I feel as if something is wrong! It is all about balance. I always try to channel nervous energy into positive thoughts, remembering that I am excited (positive), not scared (negative). I remind myself that I am lucky to be living the life I've always wanted, and I am grateful to have the opportunity to perform. I do some pre-performance yoga stretching and breathing and lie quietly for a while, trying to visualize realistically how the show will proceed. In other words, I don't imagine myself doing quadruple pirouettes. I visualize the clean doubles I have executed in rehearsals, and I don't envision worst case scenarios, such as falling or getting injured. I think about the choreography, the music, the excitement, the energy, and how much I enjoy the dance.

One of the hardest things dancers are expected to do is conquer their emotions. Publicly it's our duty to appear cool, calm, and collected, regardless of how we are feeling on the inside. With this in mind, it helps to recognize when it is time to take a mental break. Ballet is extremely taxing on the brain as well as the body. If we constantly wear ourselves thin to the point of exhaustion, we have little resistance left for handling undulating emotions.

Daily pressures of competition, perfectionism, criticism, and the scrutiny that surrounds us can be overwhelming at times, and I have seen several dancers give up on their careers just to alleviate the tension that these stressors bring on. No matter how gorgeous one's body may be in movement, if one's mind is not emotionally prepared to survive our unique environment it can spell trouble. Edward Villella's famous catchphrase is: "Ballet is a mind-driven physicality." Dancers and audiences alike have heard him say this over and over again. Though he normally uses the words in reference to movement and technique, I like to think they apply at several different levels to handling ballet. We can only progress, learn, and handle as much as our minds drive us and allow us to do.

Dancers will always struggle with days when they're feeling down, tired, unmotivated, burned out, and just "blah." We all experience it; it is normal and human. Sometimes, pushing to go to class and work through those feelings can be helpful. Focusing on class or rehearsals can actually give the mind a temporary break from external stressors, such as homework or school, and leave one feeling revived and more energized. Endorphins released through movement can help boost mood and calm down a system working on overdrive. If physical weariness is to blame, making time for a relaxing activity on an upcoming day off (a massage, a picnic in the park, an afternoon at the movies) can help get one through an especially tough week. Whatever it takes, we all need a break sometimes. Dancers all suffer from occasional "laziness." No guilt necessary—we all have our moments, and they pass. When I try to conquer those moments and channel the reduced energy efficiently and positively, I always end up feeling empowered afterward. (*Note:* If you're feeling overwhelmingly down or negative on a regular basis, there may be something more serious going on. Talk to your parents and teachers to help you figure out what may be at the root of these feelings. Let them help guide you to a solution. Remember, dancing for *yourself*, because *you* love it, should be the unwavering motivator of your passion.)

If the joy you once had in dancing seems to be lost, it is in your own best interests to try to figure out why. Remember, there is always a solution. Dr. Millie Figueredo is a professional psychologist regularly available to lend a sympathetic ear to MCB dancers and school students when necessary. When approached by dancers feeling overwhelmingly troubled, stressed, or down, she helps them to evaluate the situation and figure out what their own true goals and desires really are. "I try to help them to decide for themselves whether the sacrifices that go along with ballet are really worth it for them," she says. "Sometimes dancers get too used to their routine; they become 'comfortably' wrapped up in it, even if it may not be what makes them happiest." Dr. Figueredo asks them to imagine their lives without ballet; how would they feel if it were no longer a part of them? Some realize they love it tremendously and, despite the hardships, cannot conceive of dance being eliminated from their lives. Others begin to imagine all the alternate areas of life they would suddenly be free to explore if they were not dancing. Either way, they start honestly hearing and listening to a deeper part of themselves.

Nasty daily stressors will not soon disappear from the life of a dancer, so it is up to us be creative in handling them. Carlos and I try to keep ballet talk down to a minimum outside of work. We do spend most of our lives in the studio, so the subject is bound to come up, but we try to set boundaries limiting the amount of personal time we spend focused on it. We also try to visit with our family and nondancer friends as much as possible. This can be especially refreshing. Sharing time together makes us happy, keeps us stress free, and helps us unwind after a long hard week.

Some people feel more relaxed just being alone. I too felt this way during my first years in the company. I wanted to cool off by myself on a day off; hear myself think. If that sounds like you, try curling up with a good book, renting a movie, or taking a bubble bath while listening to your favorite music. Dancing down time is the perfect opportunity to explore hobbies and other interests as well. Some girls in the company knit, others practice yoga, and some study photography for fun. I prefer creative writing, reading, and designing leotards. Some of the men in our company enjoy surfing, diving, and photography as diversions, while others cook and paint in their free time.

Miami City Ballet corps de ballet member Rebecca King has found her down-time niche working online. During off hours, she has developed and routinely updates her blog, called *Tendus under a Palm Tree*. While taking some online college courses she rediscovered her love for writing and was inspired to take up blogging as a hobby. "I spend at least eight hours a week during the season promoting my blog and working on new posts," says Rebecca. "Ballet is a very demanding career, not just physically but also mentally. Dancers have a tendency to become so consumed by their art that they don't see much of anything outside of their careers. Through my blogging, I have embarked upon a bit of a second career that provides me with an important balance in my life. My career in ballet is very important to me, but I find that I need separate projects to keep everything in perspective."

Whatever one's pastime may be, it is important to relax, unwind, and seize the chance to enjoy it. We often think we need to eat, drink, and sleep ballet to prove ourselves seriously committed to it. On the contrary! I have found that all my other life experiences have only enhanced my dancing and enriched my overall well-being. Nowhere is it written that you need a one-track mind to be a successful ballet dancer. The most successful dancers blossom as well-rounded individuals.

King agrees that serious dancers should take on alternative projects, but not to the extent that they may distract from focus in the studio: "It is very important to find a delicate balance. Because my blog focuses on the ballet world, I find that it enhances my experiences in the studios, as I see ballet from a different point of view. I think it is important as a dancer not only to keep your body healthy but also to keep your mind healthy. Exploring different ventures allows you to take a step away from the barre and focus on some different aspects of life."

Tips

❧ Nondance exercise such as yoga, walking, or swimming can be a great stress buster. Gentle physical activity releases endorphins into the body, making you feel calmer, happier, and ready to handle everyday tension. Enjoying these activities with a friend by your side can make them even more fun and relaxing.

❧ Try to take criticism in stride, and recognize what is constructive and helpful and what is not. For every person who admires your dancing, there may be another who doesn't care for it. It all boils down to a matter of taste and opinion. All you can do is dance for yourself, and for those you are able to touch. As individuals, we each have our own wonderful qualities to share. Separate yourself from negative attention that you cannot control, believe in yourself, and be proud of who you are. Even the toughest criticism can ultimately be constructive if you keep it safe in a corner of your mind, reference it as needed, and don't take it to heart.

❧ Talk things out! Confiding in a good friend or loved one if you're feeling frustrated can be an enormous relief. Hearing an outside point of view may help you put your emotions in perspective and evaluate the true severity of the situation.

❧ Dr. Figueredo recommends reading the biographies of famous dancers and speaking with experienced company dancers when feeling overwhelmed. "It can be comforting and reassuring to learn of other dancers' struggles which have led to achievement. Dancers are often their own worst critics, and it can be destructive. If they'd learn to take that perfectionism and channel it into their own positive feedback, it could serve as a 'reality check' to help them improve rather than knock them down."

MCB's Emily Bromberg discusses her favorite pastime and business, Fancy Pants USA™:

https://www.youtube.com/watch?v=tav56khxUyk

Visit Rebecca's blog, www.tendusunder apalmtree.com:

http://tendusunderapalmtree.com/

14

Ballet's Pressures and Politics

*Facing Eating Disorders, Peer Pressure,
and Sexual Harassment*

Adjusting to the political atmosphere prevalent in many ballet companies can be a difficult thing for a young dancer. There is often a well-defined ranking system; a hierarchy of sorts. Even among members of the same rank, one may encounter a "status by seniority" dynamic. In some companies, high-ranking dancers may not even speak to those "beneath" them. Such behavior is a waste of time and energy, besides being rude. I believe that social grace, etiquette, and humility are important parts of the exclusivity of being a ballet dancer. At MCB we are thankful that we enjoy a wonderfully positive working environment, which can make all the difference in the world. We feel compelled by example to respect and support one another professionally and unwaveringly; a rarity in today's ballet world. But even in the friendliest of environments, whether in a school or company, dancers may encounter pressures inflicted by peers, older dancers, staff members, and even themselves; this is simply the nature of the beast. The answer is to take control of the reins proactively and choose how to best react under such circumstances.

In school, peer pressure may surface in several different forms: pressure to be thin and diet in unhealthy ways, pressure to compete, pressure to smoke or do drugs. Sadly, peer pressure doesn't always end with the school years. Even in the professional world there is plenty of peer pressure to be found.

Among my students the most prevalent of pressures seems to be the race to be thin. The ballet aesthetic means we all know we are expected to maintain a certain look and uphold a strict physical standard. What teens often overlook is the fact that their bodies are going through a period of tremendous change, regardless of their dancing. Figures become softer, rounder, and more womanly. Menstruation begins, often bringing with it bloating and water retention. Boys are changing too; some develop more muscle mass than others, some get softer or bulkier in certain areas, and some may remain tinier or skinnier than they would like. Going through these changes can be hard to swallow for any teen, let alone dancers. I struggled with my own teenage body issues—weight gain, bloating, and breasts that humiliatingly developed in perfect succession, one sprouting months earlier than the other! I would have given anything to wear a baggy tee shirt to class and never look in the mirror. These changes often spark one's desire to regain control. Though commiserating with peers going through similar struggles may be comforting, it can all too often lead to a dangerously competitive frame of mind. Eating disorders are a reality of the dance world that are uncomfortable to discuss but cannot be ignored.

When young dancers are struggling with physical image, self-esteem, or weight-related issues, psychologist Dr. Millie Figueredo finds it helpful to engage them in an ongoing dialogue, educating them and helping them to develop a sympathetic awareness about the biological changes coming over their bodies. She encourages them decipher both "how" and "why" they eat. *What are their usual eating habits? Are poor eating habits possibly linked to nerves or to stress? Do they seem to be eating for comfort or truly for nutrition?* "I help them try to evaluate, recognize, and understand what *their* individual body actually needs, and help them understand that while there are certain aesthetic standards to strive for, comparing themselves physically to other girls is useless. Everyone is different. Frequent comparisons usually lead to low self-esteem and diminished confidence."

Another objectionable issue quietly sneaking around the dance world is that of sexual harassment. This topic can be one of the hardest to pinpoint and recognize and one of the most awkward to discuss openly. Physical and emotional harassment and abuses can occur on several different levels: teacher-student, as frequently reported in the news and a risk pertaining in academic schools as well; director-dancer, as in Darren Aronofsky's psycho-ballet thriller *Black Swan*; or even dancer-dancer, as a problematic kind of peer pressure.

Students matriculating in the public school system are

routiney taught (usually in health or physical education classes) how to recognize and properly address situations that seem inappropriate, should they encounter these. Parents need to do their part in educating children about these potential situations as well, not just for ballet but for life in general. Respect is a two-way street and should be a reciprocal courtesy, no matter with whom you are working. If a precarious event occurs, stopping an aggressor with a firm "no," removing oneself from the situation quickly, and immediately telling a parent, trusted teacher, or higher authority are the steps for remedying the situation.

Harassment in the dance world can be slightly harder to recognize than it is elsewhere. Dance itself, especially where partnering and teaching are concerned, can be very personal and intimate, and it involves significant emotional and physical contact. Though the boundaries can sometimes get blurred, they definitely do exist. There is a line between what is appropriate and acceptable and what simply is not. It is unacceptable for a dancer ever to be purposely touched inappropriately, verbally harassed in a sexual manner, or pressured to behave in ways that make him or her feel uncomfortable. Hollywood exaggeration aside, in real life these are surely *not* a part of a ballet dancer's job description and should absolutely *not* be tolerated if ever encountered.

Uncomfortable and potentially dangerous situations are best avoided in the first place. At MCB and the MCB school, for example, studios are open for general viewing with windows all around. Company dancers are not permitted to date students, regardless of age. There is also an open-door policy practiced in both the company and the school. Dancers are welcome to visit with and alert their respective directors should they encounter any such issues. Dr. Figueredo recommends choosing "schools and companies that have both open-door policies and open facilities. These will help to prevent sexual harassment issues from ever arising, and will lower the risk of verbal, physical and emotional abuses as well." In regard to young dancers and private coaching sessions, she suggests that to discourage potentially inappropriate behaviors, "parents try to be present and attend rehearsals, or request to watch through a window if in-studio viewing is not permitted."

Company dancers may feel especially pressured to condone inappropriate behaviors or swallow objectionable advances in the hope of "getting ahead." If they are new to the company they may also fear "causing drama" through registering a protest. They may just feel they must to do what it takes to fit in. Dr. Figueredo warns that this "goes back to the issue of examining one's self-esteem and garnering strength to uphold one's integrity. Dancers all want to get ahead, but at what price? Is compromising yourself really worth it? Is it necessary? I don't think so."

(*Note:* Should you find yourself in an uncomfortable or distasteful circumstance, remove yourself as quickly as possible. Ideally, dancers should go to an authority on the company staff to put these advances to rest. If this is not an option, find a senior dancer, an outside friend, or a mentor to confide in who may be able to offer some help, support, and advice.)

Tip

Whether student or professional, a lot of the pressures, criticism, and abuse we endure is actually self-inflicted. Our pursuit of an elusive ideal, an unattainable perfection, can become a huge burden to bear. We subject ourselves daily to constant comparisons, relentless critique, endless self-evaluation, and perpetual competition; the list goes on. It can be daunting, but when we empower ourselves to turn these aggressive stressors into positives rather than negatives, they can actually help us to advance and flourish. "Because dancers constantly strive to be the best, they push—that's their drive," says Figueredo. "It's actually a positive, not a negative. Dancers critiquing their own strengths and weaknesses should try to be realistic. When people can really recognize their own weaknesses they can work on them and get better—as long as they don't allow themselves to get stuck in a negative frame of mind. They stand to benefit from being open to the idea of working steadily and improving every day, step by step." If handled this way, self-criticism, evaluation, and perfectionism can ultimately be very rewarding.

MCB's Skyler Lubin and Nathalia Arja discuss moving up in the company and handling daily pressures:

http://www.youtube.com/watch?v=CIJz6cx1Z4o

15

Stage Savvy

Understanding the Chaos behind the Curtain

Onstage at the Filene Center of the Wolf Trap National Park for the Performing Arts, right in the middle of an afternoon dress rehearsal for one of my first performances on tour with MCB, I heard a familiar voice come out of the speakers in the wings. It was the voice of the ballet mistress, loud enough to be heard well over the music. At first she had a pleasantly calm tone. "Jennifer, watch quarter please," she said.

Not quite understanding what she meant (I had my hands full counting out the music *and* trying to execute the steps—imagine!), I didn't respond very quickly. I kept dancing, wondering if perhaps someone had dropped some change that she wanted me to pick up. Then the voice came again, only louder this time: "Jennifer, *out to quarter please.*" Now I started to get nervous; she obviously wanted me to go some-where, but I hadn't a clue what she was talking about.

"Jennifer Kronenberg! Move out to quarter mark, you are too close to center!" Quickly I moved a few feet over to my right, but I had no idea where I was supposed to stop. Then I heard another voice: "*Psst*, opposite me, on the mark!" whispered the dancer across the stage from me. Which mark? There were several! Some were yellow, some were red, and others were white. Some were straight lines, and some looked like an X. "Which one?" I whispered back in a panic, but it was too late. The stage manager had already made her way onto the stage and physically pointed out the mark on which I was supposed to be. Everyone giggled, but I was mortified and on the verge of tears.

I had no idea that the stage was divided into equal eighths, marked off by different colored tape, nor that I would be responsible for dancing in a specific, exact spot at certain times. This was just the first of many new things I would have to learn about dancing onstage in the theater, especially being in the corps de ballet.

An evening at the ballet is a fascinating event; the lights go dim, the harmonious sound of the orchestra fills the theater, and the plush velvet curtain slowly rises on what seems a magical scene. A sea of beautiful, porcelain-perfect ballerinas whirl and twirl. They skim effortlessly across the stage, changing seamlessly from one formation to another. It can be almost hypnotizing, the way they move through space to the music, in unison, as smooth and lovely as a beautiful dream.

What the audience members and even new dancers don't always realize is that there is another entertaining show that goes on in the theater as well; the organized chaos that takes place *before* the curtain goes up on that picturesque wonderland. Many people don't appreciate how much detailed teamwork goes into creating something so lovely. A ballet production is like a well-oiled machine with countless parts working together to create the final production.

Though the dancers get most of the credit at the end of the show, the magic of the ballet would not exist without the director and ballet mistresses, stage manager and stage hands, lighting designer and technicians, audio technician, wardrobe master, prop master, carpenter, and of course the conductor and musicians. When all these people pull together, the result is flawless. If anyone slacks off or doesn't follow direction properly, however, it can instantly lead to chaos.

Dancers are primarily responsible for taking direction from the artistic director, ballet mistress, and stage manager. Before the dancing starts, there can be a lot of tension, anxiety, and nerves. With everyone running around trying to prepare and go over last minute details, it is necessary that dancers have a clear understanding of what their responsibilities are and from whom they should be taking direction. Once that curtain rises, the stage manager's voice is the one to which performers should be paying attention. That is the voice that keeps the dancers and all the other parts of the machine working together in unison until the curtain goes back down.

While a performance is in progress, the stage manager is responsible for *everyone* in that space: keeping everyone on schedule, facilitating the needs of each particular performance or stage rehearsal, and looking out for everyone's safety and well-being. "We are like an air traffic controller in a major airport," says Nicolle Mitchell, stage manager for Miami City Ballet. There are so many different artists and crew members involved in putting on a production, all with different needs, responsibilities, and information to contribute; it's like having several airplanes landing and taking off in an airport all at once. Needing coordination are dancers, designers, ballet mistresses or masters, directors, wardrobe people, prop handlers, sound technicians, musicians, conductors, electricians, spotlight operators, staff from the venue, and more. "As the stage manager, I need to know what all these people do during the performance, when they're supposed to do it, and what they'll need to accomplish their tasks successfully. I then guide them through the event so that there are no 'collisions,' so to speak, making sure that the performance or rehearsal runs as smoothly and seamlessly as possible." As a dancer, it is *very* important to communicate openly with the stage manager, who should be aware of any needs or concerns so as to be able to fix any potential problems. Performers should *always* heed any information their stage manager relays to them; there is always a good reason behind it, though it may not always be clear at the moment.

The easiest way to refer to the happenings on different parts of the stage at any given time is by dividing the stage up into equal fractional sections. If a dancer is not in a particular place at a specific time, lighting and music cues can go wrong, and in the worst case scenario, collisions could happen with other dancers or with scenery flying in and out. I once watched a scenery backdrop get lowered onto a dancer's head because he was standing in the wrong spot at the wrong moment! Studying the dimensions of the stage, and knowing which colors one's company or school uses to identify each division, will ensure that dancers are prepared to take in and follow stage directions properly when given.

According to Mitchell, the biggest "crimes" she has seen dancers commit in the theater are bringing coffee and food onstage or onto the backstage area or "deck," and making noise backstage during the performance. "Hearing dancers yell 'Bravo!' and making noise from the wings is distracting to both audience and performers, and is just unprofessional. Though it is wonderful to support one another, there is an appropriate time and place for it. The performance is ultimately for the audience's enjoyment, not our own gratification. There is a delicate web created when the performers onstage connect in such a strong way that the audience is completely engrossed in what is happening. By making noise, you run the risk of breaking that web. Your fellow dancers and the audience can easily be pulled out of that moment."

Fluency in stage etiquette, rules, and language is mandatory. It allows a dancer to contribute to any production more efficiently and effectively, creating the fantasy world that people buy their tickets to see. Ballet production is a true team effort comparable to professional football or basketball, only the end result is more decorous.

Tips

෨ Scope out each stage and backstage area before your first dress rehearsal. Every venue is different. Marks may be closer or farther apart, and there may be more or fewer of them, depending on the ballet, the dimensions of the stage, and the amount of scenery. The number and depth of the wings in different theaters also varies, and there may or may not be a crossover on deck. Being aware of any differences ahead of time allows a smoother dress or stage rehearsal, and allows you to focus on what is most important—dancing!

෨ Should you encounter a slippery stage (some surfaces may be more worn than others, and some linoleum panels may offer less cushioning than you expect), ask ahead of time if using rosin is permitted. If not, no need to panic. There are other ways to prevent slip-and-fall accidents. Using a little water to dampen the tips and soles of your shoes provides some extra "stick" (this trick works especially well for gentlemen who wear canvas shoes since the fabric easily will absorb and retain the moisture). Be careful, though; less is definitely more. Too much water in the wrong places can damage or ruin pointe shoes. Since the tacky effect of the water wears off quickly, keep a moistened cloth or sponge in the wings to reapply between entrances. Another option is to request that the floor be mopped with Slip NoMor, a slip-resistant solution for dance flooring, or a little bit of cola if no other solution is readily available. Since cola is extremely sticky, this is usually done only sparingly and in response to severe or dangerous circumstances. One more possible step is scuffing up the soles of your pointe shoes with a cheese grater, rasping tool, or scissors (be very careful!) to provide better traction. In addition to scraping my shoes, I always come prepared with a super-soft pair just in case, as these tend to be less slippery. If all else fails, I'll bang out my pre-hardened shoes on a concrete surface, making them quieter, softer, and less likely to catch an edge and slip.

Backstage Basics

1. Be on time! Be at the theater and sign yourself in at least one half hour prior to show time to assure production staff that you are available and ready to perform, even if you are not scheduled to dance that evening. Also, be on-stage in your costume, shoes on and ready to go, at least five minutes before curtain time.

2. Try to wear black or dark-colored warmers while standing backstage. Try to remain as inconspicuous as possible should the audience be able to see into the wings (stage hands are always dressed in black for this reason).

3. Cover your ballet shoes with socks or booties while walking around the theater. Any wax or debris picked up by your shoes can be tracked onto the stage, causing slippery spots!

4. *Be quiet!* Always keep talking to a minimum, and keep your voice down to a low whisper. The audience can hear

chatter going on backstage. We are hidden behind a fabric curtain, not a brick wall.

5. If you want to clap for your fellow dancers, take your cue from the audience. Backstage clapping, whooping, and hollering should *never* precede or be louder than that which is coming from the house.

6. *Never* eat, drink, sit on the floor, or smoke in costume! Some companies will fine you for breaking this rule. (Better yet, don't smoke at all.)

7. Clean up after yourself; throw away all used tissues, bandage wrappers, etc., in appropriate receptacles. They can get stuck to shoes and costumes and be tracked onto the stage if left on the floor.

8. Don't stand directly in front of the side lights in the wings; doing so will create a shadow of you on stage. (Always walk *behind* the upstage footlights for the same reason.)

9. *Never* bring any food or drink onto the stage or stage deck. Water in a closed bottle is the only liquid ever permitted.

10. Do not bring your cell phone or pager onto the stage deck. It will surely ring at the very worst moment!

11. Remember that "upstage" means toward the back of the stage, and "downstage" means toward the audience. (Stages used to be raked, or slanted, making the back higher up than the front.)

12. Review your steps onstage before the show to reassure yourself of the space and marks. This is especially helpful

when sets are involved, to make sure that they are in their proper place *before* the show starts. Stagehands can make mistakes too.

13. Always double check your own costumes and props. Do not rely on others to place them for you, or they may not be where you need them to be during the show. Wardrobe and crew have many props and costumes to think about and cannot always keep track of everyone and everything. If you realize something is missing, alert the stage manager in a timely fashion so as to get the problem fixed promptly. *Never* play with or move costumes and props that aren't yours. By doing so, you can inadvertently cause an emergency situation.

14. Unless it is an emergency, do not disturb a stage manager who is calling cues into a headset. Not only can your voice be heard by everyone else also on headset, causing confusion, but important cues could be missed if the stage manager gets distracted. Instead, speak to an assistant, or wait for an appropriate moment to garner the stage manager's attention.

15. Clear the stage deck as promptly as possible following a performance and in between ballets. Time is of the essence when changing the stage from one ballet to the next, and if you are in the way the process is delayed. It can also be dangerous. Always listen, be aware, and react quickly—if someone from the crew is telling you to move, it is usually for a very good reason!

Our Friends behind the Scenes

Technical director—Oversees everything and everyone in the production, including the stage manager; also referred to as the production director.

Stage manager—Responsible for pulling the entire production together; ensures the show runs smoothly from beginning to end.

Head carpenter—In charge of all set pieces and backdrops; bring the main curtain in and out.

Properties head—In charge of every prop a dancer handles on stage and of the floor, portable barres for class, rosin, and sewing boxes; also known as the prop master.

Electricians—In charge of all stage lights and spotlights and anything onstage powered by electricity (e.g., fog machines, Nutcracker Christmas tree).

Sound engineer—Controls the balance and volume of music onstage, in the house, and in the orchestra pit; may be in charge of videography as well.

Wardrobe master or mistress—Takes care of tights, undergarments, shoes, all costumes, headpieces, etc.

16

It's Not Just for Girls!

Bravo for Boys in Ballet

It is a terrific shame that in the twenty-first century many people in the United States still believe that ballet is just for girls, and sports are for boys. What a terrible misconception—especially since some of the greatest athletes and superstars of our time are male ballet dancers who grew up here in the United States, came here to complete their training, or ventured here to expand their own career opportunities. Take for example the celebrated Mikhail Baryshnikov, who quickly found himself elevated to superstar status in this country because of his immense dancing talents. The documentary *Born to Be Wild* provides a great example of some of the strongest male dancers of this generation: Jose Manuel Carreño, Ethan Stiefel, Vladimir Malakhov, and Angel Corella. Though their childhoods differed tremendously—(one grew up in Cuba, one in Russia, one in Spain, and one was a motorcycle-riding all-American guy)—they all made fantastically successful careers for themselves. After years of success as principal dancers of the American Ballet Theater, three now split their time between dancing and directing schools and companies. Stiefel was featured as the star of the movie *Center Stage*. He was chosen for the role because of his celebrity as ballet dancer.

Edward Villella is perhaps the most famous of "ultra-masculine" American male dancers. He grew up playing baseball on the streets of Queens, New York, until he was unwillingly dragged to his sister's ballet lessons. At first he thought ballet was just for girls and sissies. How quickly his point of view changed when the *grand allegro* (big jumping combinations) started. He suddenly fell in love with the athleticism! Ballet presented new physical challenges and an excitement that he hadn't discovered before. When he left the dance to go off to a maritime college, he ended up missing it terribly. He later returned to ballet, and through a lot of hard work and sweat he continued to a wonderful career as a principal dancer with New York City Ballet. Years after his performing career ended, he became founding artistic director of Miami City Ballet.

If you are a boy training in ballet today, I applaud you! A bizarre stigma is constantly associated with boys in dance, making many afraid to try it. Some won't even admit that they like to watch it for fear of being teased, taunted, and bullied. This just baffles me. As Villella would surely attest, there is nothing even remotely ridiculous about the sheer strength, athleticism, and masculinity of many male dancers. He was himself a welterweight boxing champion and won a letter on the varsity baseball team before he ever danced professionally. These sports may have contributed to the strength and speedy dancing for which he became known. And let's not forget that female dancers are dependent on the leading men. Even the loveliest Juliet will not get very far without a powerful, reliable Romeo dancing behind her. We truly appreciate our strong male partners; and we definitely count on them.

Though American minds are slowly beginning to broaden, our culture still leads many to presume that boys do not have an honorable place in ballet. We stand almost alone in this narrow-minded belief. In Russia, Europe, and Japan, for example, it is considered a triumph to be a ballet dancer, whether male or female. In Cuba, superb male dancers are created by the dozens! In fact, their schools practically specialize in male training. What a shame that male dancing is not yet as celebrated here in our own country.

To those who have ignored society, begun their ballet training, and are not ashamed of enjoying it, bravo! Individuality and conviction are valiant qualities. Be proud of them! I imagine many gentlemen have the same questions and concerns as their female counterparts. Generally speaking, most of the subjects discussed in the earlier chapters apply to males as well. There are a few areas, however, of which gentlemen will need to be aware, where specific information should differ slightly from that directed toward the ladies. My husband, Carlos, has helped me to address these issues from a male dancer's perspective.

The most important issue he thought it necessary to discuss is injury prevention. While girls suffer most of their injuries in their feet, ankles, and hips, boys are more prone to knee, back, and shoulder injuries as a result of all of the high-impact jumping and lifting required of them. Special attention should be paid to strengthening the deep inner muscles supporting these areas. Weight training is usually an elective for boys in larger ballet schools, but one must be very cautious in one's approach to this kind of work. It is not necessarily a safe thing to begin early on in one's training, and the weights lifted should not be so heavy as to build bulky muscle mass, which can hinder dancing. Male dancers need strong, elongated, and lean muscle tone, allowing for both partnering stability and fluidity of movement. Lifting weights that are too heavy and using incorrect lifting techniques can actually cause lower back injuries, instead of preventing them.

In lieu of early weight lifting, Carlos suggests that his younger male students try Pilates training using the arm straps on a reformer, which creates resistance tension using coiled springs and is easily adjusted to suit each user. Gyrotonic® training is another wonderful method for guys to strengthen their core, shoulder girdle, and back muscles using a circular motion and weight resistance that in many ways mimics the way a dancer dances. The kettlebell training method is also beneficial for boys in its unique use of weight, dynamics, and momentum to develop stability in the shoulder girdle. When the weights are swung correctly, using momentum generated by the legs, it actually simulates the way one would lift a ballerina and react to her constantly shifting weight and movements. Training with the bells can really help improve one's partnering skills. Not only will dancers practice counterbalancing while reacting to the bells' resistance in motion, but they will also practice proper techniques necessary to control a ballerina's takeoff and landing from lifts. Propulsion from the legs must be used to propel the weight up, but the legs must also be used to cushion the strong gravitational pull on the way down.

Carlos recommends the no-frills, boot camp–type conditioning that boys studying ballet are made to do back in his country, Cuba. Push-ups, pull-ups, planks (great for the arms, pectoral chest muscles, and abdominals), sit-ups (mainly targeting the abs), and squats (wonderful for the quadriceps and hamstrings) all use one's own body weight to develop strength, stability, and endurance. But his favorite training technique is one he just can't seem to escape: press lifting—me, that is—right over his head in our rehearsals each day.

Gentlemen must also remember that it is important for them to stretch. Men's muscles tend to be a bit more compact in structure than women's, so active daily stretching after classes or at the end of a rehearsal day is a must. Carlos is naturally quite flexible, but he still dedicates at least half an hour to stretching his legs, arms, feet, and back at the end of each work day. He recommends stretching only after class, when the muscles are very warm. "Active" stretching (such as lunges) before class can be beneficial, but it is best to do an alternative cardio warm-up first. Crunches, brisk walking or jogging, or bicycle riding are all good ways to get one's blood pumping to muscles and joints.

Physical therapists normally recommend that when

stretching, dancers spend about thirty seconds specifically focused on stretching each muscle group, for about three to four repetitions. Elasticity of the muscles is important for achieving a beautiful line of the body—especially in typical male steps such as *grand jeté* (a long horizontal jump), and *coupé jeté* (a cutting action preceded by a long horizontal jump, usually done traveling around in a circle)—and, all things considered, will surely enhance a man's dancing. (*Note:* Be careful and gentle; overstretching, holding or sitting in stretches for too long, or stretching when cold can quickly lead to injury.)

Tip

✎ If there aren't many older boys, men, or company dancers in your school environment to look up to or watch, do some research on your own. Surf the Internet for video clips and photos. Order, download, or borrow from the public library DVDs, books, and videos of ballets you like and dancers you admire. Watching them as an example can be a fantastic inspiration. Study what it is that specifically draws you to each particular dancer, and try to emulate and incorporate these qualities into your own dancing.

MCB male dancers Shimon Ito, Klebber Rebello, and Carlos Miguel Guerra share their different experiences discovering and exploring their love for dance:

http://www.youtube.com/watch?v=P6wbuuC-pTk

17

Stability vs. Variety

Company Work, Freelancing, and Agents

In my eighteen years of employment with the same ballet company I have seen many a dancer come and go. As I approached my place at the barre for the first time at MCB, I sensed right away that I was at home. I felt fulfilled and constantly challenged from my very first season as an apprentice. In one singular company I have continually discovered new motivation, incentive, and a broad platform to develop my career steadily. With artistic peace of mind, I was able to settle down, build a life for myself, and call Miami home. Without a doubt, and to the dismay of some of my wilder friends, I've always been a lover of comfort and stability. I always know when my next paycheck will be, and how much it will be, allowing me to budget my life accordingly.

For several dancers, however, stability can be equated with monotony and can trigger boredom. If not recognized, this may easily wreak havoc on one's career. Some dancers will not thrive following a clear-cut day-to-day routine and may feel stifled dancing ballets that revolve cyclically through a company's permanent repertoire. I know quite a few dancers who continuously crave the rush of being in a new and exciting work environment, experimenting with different styles and discovering new outlooks. For many, the idea of working in small groups, in close connection with new choreographers, and being part of specialized workshops is very appealing, and others yearn for the ongoing opportunity to tour and travel around the globe on a regular basis. For this type of dancer personality, freelancing can be incredibly gratifying.

Do keep in mind, however, that as exciting as it may sound, regular freelancing can also mean dealing with insecurity, instability, and at times even hardship. The technical definition of a freelancer is a person who sells services without working on a regular basis for any single employer. This can mean that as a freelancer, one may risk forfeiting eligibility to collect government-funded unemployment compensation benefits and services. (This benefit is usually earned through maintaining substantial full-time employment for at least one full year, and is collected by most dancers to help them through the yearly off-season, when we are not paid.) Dancers may also find themselves confronted with the need to purchase an independent health insurance plan (if no longer eligible to be covered by the plan of a parent, guardian, or family member), and may have to build their own retirement funds independently through an individual retirement account, or

IRA. Freelancing can mean going for months without an offer of dancing work, and the need may arise to take on other jobs to make ends meet.

Successful freelancers must be extremely self-motivated. They are regularly on the hunt for their next "gig" and must be willing to check call boards and magazines constantly for posted audition notices, to network with dancer friends, and to become familiar with marketing themselves through Web and social media forums. Many find it easier and less daunting to secure work through the help of an agent; but this help normally comes with a price tag. Ballet agents have been known to charge fees of anywhere between 10 and 30 percent (calculated from a dancer's earnings, per contract) for finding and providing a dancer with freelance work. Not only do they help find the job for the dancer, but they also arrange travel, take care of contract negotiations, and any handle any other logistics that dancers may not feel comfortable dealing with on their own.

Professional dance agent Todd Fox co-created Elitedance.com and Elitedance Artists Management back in 1999. Through his agency he helps professional dancers acquire supplemental dancing work. He is an agent who solely represents guest artist ballet dancers, securing them short-term performance engagements that meet specific artistic and financial standards set forth by his clients. Once an offer for employment has been obtained, he then works with the employer to forge a legally binding agreement covering all his client's individual and professional requirements. As the performance engagement approaches, he monitors arrangements and makes sure of the follow-through on everything detailed in the contract.

Each agent has a particular set of priorities, so dancers must make sure that these are in line with their own before committing to and acquiring an agent's services. Fox says, "Safety is always my number one priority when sending out a client and is something I never negotiate or compromise. My next priority is negotiating a fair salary commensurate with my client's background, ability, and potential audience draw. Last but not least is to document how well my client's needs were met while out on the engagement and to evaluate the employer for future clients."

Some agents tend to be choosy about the clientele they take on, so dancers should do their research well and pick out a few who may be a good fit. Agents may ask for a video if they've never seen a particular dancer perform, and they will most definitely want an up-to-date photo and résumé. For Fox, considering a ballet dancer for representation is based primarily on two factors—work ethic and experience, in that order. "A ballet dancer's work ethic is the most important detail because my reputation as an agent and that of all the dance artists I represent is on the line when I send a client out on a performance engagement," he said. "It only takes one bad experience, and an employer will simply seek out another agent to fulfill future guest artist needs, and that affects every artist I represent. I personally check up on every dancer whom I consider for representation."

Fox suggests that dancers have all their background information (résumé/CV, images, video clips, etc.) in proper order before seeking out representation or work as a freelance ballet dancer. After all, these are the first things that will be requested when being considered for employment, and they may be needed at a moment's notice. Elitedance Artists Management and other agencies usually prefer traditional methods for submitting professional information (i.e., printed materials sent by regular mail or e-mail files in standard formats). Including a personal message regarding the reason for submission is also a plus. (*Note: Never* instruct any agent or potential employer to view your Facebook page or to Google your name to review your background experience. This is considered unprofessional and unacceptable by most. Be aware, however, that they may very well do so on their own, so be sure to keep your Internet presence as "clean" and respectable as possible.) Following up with an employer or agent once materials have been submitted can be especially helpful for obtaining feedback that may help you improve future submissions.

Communication is always the key, so have an open dialogue with agents about their specific fees and requirements. One must also be straightforward about one's schedule and availability—especially important if already under contract with a company with a clear-cut schedule to follow. A partnership is being created, so the more up front and honest a dancer is from the get-go, the better. It is also essential to be accessible for timely communication. Ballet life can get busy and hectic, but dancers must make themselves available to be reached within a matter of hours if they expect the agent-client relationship to be successful. "Things can move very quickly in this business," says Fox, and "opportunities can sometimes slip through your fingers in a matter of hours if communication between agent and client is slow or lacking." Excuses are simply not acceptable.

Sporadic freelancing (or "guesting") can also be a wonderful outlet for full-time company dancers who are modestly in search of more performing opportunities, teaching experience, or a way to earn some extra cash during their company's layoff period. My husband, Carlos, and I fall under this category. MCB offers its dancers between thirty-five and forty-two weeks of employment per contracted season (not bad for a ballet company in the United States), but that still leaves us an average of about two months during which we have no guaranteed source of income. This can be worrisome when you've got a bunch of bills to pay. They don't go away, whether we're employed or not. Our agents help us to find temporary employment during that time frame and also during the holidays—better known as *Nutcracker* time. Since we are constantly performing with MCB, these are the only intervals during which we are available to do extra outside work. It definitely keeps us calm knowing that we have someone helping us to secure dancing and teaching employment well in advance of those relatively predictable off periods. For us, an agent's fee seems a small price to pay for that peace of mind.

Ballerina Marife Gimenez chose to explore the world of full-time freelancing after years dancing with several different companies, including Miami City Ballet, Ballet Nacional de Caracas, Maximum Dance Company, and Ballet Florida. She warns: "Freelancing will allow a dancer tremendous freedom, but it also brings with it a lot of responsibility and work that dancers don't normally have to worry about while in a company. True artistic fulfillment in either is really dependent on the personality of the dancer." Gimenez successfully secured several engagements with Ballet Pacifica, L.A. Ballet, New Orleans Ballet Theater, and other companies. While she says that "the money you can potentially make is very enticing, and the freedom to perform different styles can make a dancer grow much faster artistically," she urges that a dancer should ideally secure the right contacts to find abundant work before taking the freelancing plunge. "This will not only help one earn money consistently enough to survive, but also avoids the physical stress of being 'in and out' of performing shape in between gigs."

Tips

 ☙ If and when you do accept a guesting opportunity, be sure that all contract terms and payment arrangements are specified in writing up front. Take special note of whether shoes, tights, costumes, music, etc. are provided or if you as the guest artist are expected to supply them. And don't forget to bring your own supply of rosin! Often, stages and rehearsal floors are hard and slippery. Try to prevent an accident before it happens by having your own stash of rosin ready to go. I like to have a line in the contract stating that *I, as the artist, shall be permitted to use rosin on the performance floor as needed and at my own professional discretion*, just to be on the safe side. In some theaters the use of rosin is prohibited, and this is a challenge for which I like to be prepared before I go, rather than being surprised with it when I arrive.

~ Before deciding to work with an agent, be sure to talk to your director (school or company) and get well acquainted with what the guesting policies are. Some companies, like MCB for instance, will only release dancers ranked soloist and above for guesting opportunities, and then only during *Nutcracker* season. Other companies that have lighter performance schedules, or fewer contracted weeks, may allow their dancers freedom to guest much more regularly. As far as schools go, some may feel favorably about their advanced students accepting performance opportunities (paid or not), and others may frown upon it. In any case, make sure you are familiar with the rules of your institution sooner, rather than later!

18

It's Not Just for the Pros!

The Joy of Ballet Is for Anyone

Through all my years of training I could never relate to my fellow classmates who were doing it "just for fun." Of course, I enjoyed dancing tremendously too, but my joy led me to a very serious level of commitment. I couldn't understand how anyone could study ballet casually for sheer joy, grace, or just plain physical exercise, without any intention of becoming a professional. I realize now just how silly I was.

In every advanced class of pre-professional-level students, only a handful will continue to a performing career. For starters, there simply are not enough job opportunities to accommodate all who are interested in the field. Not all dedicated students have professionalism in mind as their ultimate goal, either. One might wonder if so many years of hard work and dedication are worthwhile when the odds of "making it" are so unpredictable. The answer is, undeniably, *yes*.

Ballet training offers an unparalleled level of challenge, discipline, and self-awareness to those who undertake it.

(I think the only practice that may offer a comparable array of qualities is the study of martial arts.) It is also one of the few extremely demanding physical practices that, on a nonprofessional level, can continually be restructured to suit the needs of the dancer. This unique quality enables those who enjoy it to continue practicing throughout their lives, from early childhood well into mature adulthood. Numerous open-enrollment adult ballet classes are currently offered throughout the country, in which one can find students ranging from teenagers to the elderly, each adjusting the class intensity level to fit individual capabilities and goals.

From the very start, ballet instills a sense of grace and dignity in those who study it. Some of the first things taught are poise, posture, respect, and discipline, which all prove extremely useful in other areas of life and study. Posture and poise alone often set those who have studied ballet apart in a crowd. The grace with which dancers carry themselves tends to make them appear more confident and self-assured than the average person.

The respect and discipline necessary to succeed as a ballet student also work wonders in other aspects of life; particularly in school! I know my intense capability to focus, absorb, and memorize (skills I practiced daily in ballet) were duly noted and appreciated by my academic teachers. I benefited from an advanced understanding in music appreciation class as well as some knowledge of French for my foreign language class. I also managed to tutor myself in some of the harder subjects, like physics and geometry, by relating what I was learning in these subjects to ballet steps. After all, ballet is full of jumps, turns, and partnering, which all adhere to the laws of physics, and all its poses and positions are based on geometric shapes and angles.

There are other career paths that involve dance as well, and ballet training will eventually come in handy for most of them. Teaching and choreographing are the most obvious, but one could also branch out into areas such as stage production or costume design. Our physical therapists at Miami City Ballet are both trained in ballet, as are some of the greatest dance photographers and critics around the world. The possibilities are many.

Perhaps the greatest advantage to studying ballet is of the physical kind. Dancing ballet is undoubtedly an excellent form of exercise. Students become extremely attuned to their bodies and often retain the desire to preserve their physical health and well-being into adulthood. Physical fitness and maintenance are generally lacking in the world today. Ballet classes offer a creative, fun, and affordable way for those who enjoy it to reap the benefits of daily exercise that enhances their strength, flexibility, coordination, and cardiovascular health.

Bottom line: ballet is for anyone who loves and appreciates dancing. People who enjoy it should stick with it, even if professional dancing may not be in their future. As long as one is realistic about one's goals, ballet training has scores of wonderful benefits to offer—innumerable rewards that will continue to be reaped throughout life, dance career or not.

Tip

≋ Do not let anyone or anything take away your love of the dance! Dancing is a wonderful form of expression physically, artistically, and intellectually. It can put you in touch with your truest feelings and deepest emotions if you allow this. It is a gift that anyone and everyone should feel free to experience. Professionalism is truly wonderful, if that's the track you find yourself on, but recreational, nonprofessional dancing can be very rewarding as well. Be true to yourself and you'll undoubtedly find the path that is right for you.

19

Money Matters—Be Financially Prepared

Layoffs, Unemployment, and Retirement Funds

As professional dancers, we resign ourselves to the fact that we will never strike it rich in this profession. Ultimately we dance for love, not money. Still, in the real world, dancers have to find a way to survive, paying rent and bills just like everyone else. When I began as an apprentice with MCB I earned a mere $250 per week, plus a monthly $200 living stipend. Though the cost of living was certainly lower back in 1994, my salary was far from a fortune. I had to budget carefully to make ends meet. What really hit me hard was the annual layoff, during which time I would receive no pay at all. Trying to save enough money to get me through this period became a challenging headache of a mission. I also realized that I would need to start saving for my retirement. A dancer will retire about twenty years before the average citizen, meaning we can't rely on immediate Social Security benefits. Dancers employed in the United States also won't receive any sort of pension or retirement compensation from their companies. Dancers are responsible for saving their own nest egg to get them safely through from the day they stop dancing to the day that they embark on their next career. To grow to an adequate amount of money, an account needs to be started well in advance of one's estimated retirement age.

Tips

MAKING IT THROUGH LAYOFF PERIODS

❧ Create a budget and tally up how much money you actually need to live from month to month (rent, bills, groceries, etc.). Multiply this number by the number of months you will be without pay, and this is the amount of money that you will need to have available before the layoff period. Start saving week by week, little by little, from the start of the season to reach this goal. I used to "eat cheap" on tours and save all of my per diem (daily food allowance). By the end of the season, I would have saved enough money to cover at least one month's expenses.

❧ Apply for Unemployment Compensation benefits from your state to help make ends meet. Your benefit amount will be determined by your weekly salary, so it may not be much, but every little bit of money will help.

❧ Ask your company if they will pro-rate your paycheck. Your annual salary then will be divided by the fifty-two weeks in the year instead of the contracted number of work weeks, and you will be paid this amount (minus tax) year round. Though the amount of each paycheck will be less, you'll never be without one, even during the layoff period. The downside? If the company is "saving" your money for you, which is in effect what pro-rating accomplishes, then the company is earning the interest that you could be making on it. If you budget and save the money or invest it yourself, *you* could be making that interest and adding it to your savings pot!

ˣ Look for extra work during the layoff—guesting, teaching, chaperoning at a summer intensive, or any other type of temporary job.

ˣ If you live alone, consider taking on a roommate to help share expenses. Also, temporarily subletting your apartment if you plan to be away during the layoff months can help save you from paying your rent and utility bills until the season resumes.

SAVING FOR RETIREMENT

ˣ Retirement may be the furthest thing from one's mind, and it may seem quite silly to be thinking about this even before one has gotten the first job, but it is an unavoidable reality that we all find ourselves facing at some point. Most established companies provide their dancers the option of enrolling in a companywide 403(b) or 401(k) retirement plan: money is deducted from your paycheck before taxes and deposited into an investment account. If neither of these is an option (or if you are a permanent freelancer or self-employed), then setting up an individual retirement account (IRA) can be a wonderful alternative. IRAs can easily be established on an individual basis at banks, financial institutions, and investment firms. Be sure to visit one to obtain additional information. Research the possibilities well before making a choice, as every option will have several pros and cons to weigh.

∞ There are usually penalties associated with withdrawing funds from a retirement account before reaching a certain age. If you don't want to be penalized, you may want to opt to save or invest money instead in a mutual fund account, which will produce comparable interest growth but allows money to be withdrawn at any time. These accounts do not provide the same tax deferral benefits as an IRA, but they may be a more convenient option in the long run, depending on one's retirement goals.

MCB *corps de ballet* member Kara White shares her salary saving tips:

http://www.youtube.com/watch?v=A11iY88Ppr8

20

So, Is It Really Worth It?

Total Commitment to the Dance

Ballet, just like life, is a roller-coaster, a winding labyrinth of events revealing new surprises around every bend, some friendly and others terrifying. In exchange for the many splendors of ballet, all dancers surrender a piece of themselves and their innermost being over to it. I don't believe that those who are truly passionate about ballet ever get that piece of themselves back. An unbreakable bond is formed; a marriage, for better or for worse. Outsiders adoringly profess admiration for dancers, for the great sacrifices that we make for our art. Can our devotion really be considered sacrifice though, when it is our own hearts we are ultimately following? For me, it isn't a sacrifice. Rather, it is a choice; an exchange. I've given a piece of my heart over to the dance, and I have received in return an ever growing joy, an ever changing freedom, an ever expanding knowledge, and an immeasurable sense of fulfillment. Dancers are a rare species and are never truly satisfied; we are constantly searching and striving

FIGURES 39, 40. *Giselle*, Act 2. Photos courtesy of Joe Gato.

FIGURES 41, 42. George Balanchine's *Slaughter on Tenth Avenue*. © The George Balanchine Trust, photo courtesy of Leigh Esty Photos.

FIGURE 43. John Cranko's *Romeo and Juliet*, Balcony Pas de Deux.
Photo courtesy of Leigh Esty Photos.

for more. Ballet has been my sustenance, food for my soul. It has allowed me to find my own incentive, my own drive. I enter the studio each and every day to work just a little harder than the day before. Performing, growth, and contribution are my rewards.

For me, ballet has been a world of fantasy, yet one that is very tangible and real—like the last flashes of a dream just before one wakes up. One moment I'm gazing up at a satisfyingly peaceful sky and the next I'm suddenly in freefall, desperately afraid to hit the ground. Certain impressions remain vividly crystal clear, and others are hazy and easily forgotten. They slip right away, no matter how hard I try to hold onto them. Time passes both quickly and slowly, and I'm never quite sure about which side of the looking glass I'm standing on. I would never wish away my capacity to dream, even if dreams are never predictable.

Nothing that is worth doing is ever easy. As I look back on the many years past and look forward to those yet to come, I can sincerely say that the unimaginable joy and accomplishment that ballet has brought to my existence has absolutely been worth every drop of blood and sweat, and every tear that has been shed. I'll forever be able to look back and know that I have made my own dreams come true.

I am a ballerina.

Keep up with me and my career experiences or share your own experiences and questions with me and other young dancers here on my blog, www.ballerina2the pointe.com:

http://ballerina2thepointe.com/

Acknowledgments

Warm heartfelt thanks to all of my special friends, colleagues, and professional ballet dancers who contributed their thoughts, feelings, and experiences to enhance this book.

I'd like to thank the several professionals who enriched the information I've provided with their expertise, and who dedicate themselves daily to caring for and about dancers: Edward Villella; Nicolle Mitchell; Todd Fox; Millie Figueredo, PhD; Cynthia McGee Laportilla, MSPT, LMT; Ryan Sobus, MPH, RD; and Michelle Khai, BS, CSCS.

An enormous thanks to my husband and fellow dancer, Carlos Miguel Guerra, who helped me see ballet through a male perspective and inspired and helped me to write my chapter for boys.

My deep appreciation and loving thanks to my brother Matthew, who cheered me on and helped me tremendously in bringing the final stages of this book project together.

I'd also like to express my gratitude to all of the young dancers who have written to me on my blog at http://ballerina2the pointe.com in search of advice and answers. They have truly inspired me to go forth in expanding this book from its original electronic format.

JCK

Glossary

Balanchine, George (1904–1983): One of the twentieth century's most famous choreographers, a developer of ballet in the United States, and the co-founder and original ballet master of the New York City Ballet and the School of American Ballet; a choreographer who was primarily known for his intricate musicality.

Balanchine technique: The method and style of ballet developed by George Balanchine and commonly associated with the New York City Ballet and the School of American Ballet; now widely adapted across North America. Unlike the Vaganova method, the Balanchine style is not taught by way of a standardized graded training system; rather there are various methods used to teach it.

barre (n.): 1. A horizontal wooden or metal bar, at approximately waist height, used at the start of a ballet class for warm-up exercises and stretches. 2. The series of primary exercises using a bar for support and balance during a ballet class.

blister (n.): A pocket of fluid within the upper layers of the skin usually caused by friction, burning, or freezing. Some blisters can be filled with blood (blood blisters) or pus if they become infected.

bromelain (n.): An extract derived from the stems of pineapples, though existent in all parts of the plant and fruit; as a supplement it has been found to have anti-inflammatory properties and effects.

bunion (n.): The "bump" on the side of the big toe joint; the deformity is a sideways deviation of the big toe causing the tissues surrounding the joint to become swollen and tender.

callus (n.): Hard, tough area of skin that has thickened due to repeated friction, pressure, and irritation.

calories (n.): Unit used to measure and express food energy, or the amount of energy obtained from food.

calorimetry (n.): The science of measuring the heat of chemical reactions and/or physical changes; indirect calorimetry calculates the heat that living organisms produce from their production of carbon dioxide and nitrogen waste or from their consumption of oxygen.

carbohydrate (n.): Any food that is rich in the complex carbohydrate starch, such as cereal, bread, or pasta, or in simple carbohydrates, such as sugar; they are a common source of energy in living organisms.

compound tincture of benzoin (n.): A pungent solution that can be applied to the skin to protect it from allergy before applying tape and adhesive bandages; also used by athletes to toughen the skin exposed to it.

corn (n.): A specially shaped callus of dead skin that tends to form on the dorsal surfaces of toes; corns form when the pressure point against the skin traces an elliptical path during the rubbing motion. Hard corns tend to form on the dry, flat surfaces of skin (tops of toes), while soft corns stay moist (forming mainly in between toes).

coupé jeté (n.): A traveling step in which one cuts underneath oneself, makes a three-quarter turn, and completes the turn with a large splitting jump called a *grand jeté*.

electrolyte (n.): Primarily sodium, potassium, calcium, and magnesium in physiology; an aid in regulating blood PH and the hydration of the body and critical for nerve and muscle function.

en des hors (adj.): 1. The French ballet term for rotating outward, or turning out one's legs and feet. 2. Used to describe the action of actually turning to the outside, or clockwise.

en pointe (adj.): The French term dancing *en pointe* means "on one's toes"; *demi pointe* is the term used to describe the half toe or forced arch position in which men and young girls dance when not in pointe shoes.

essential fats (n.): Fats or fatty acids that humans must ingest because the body needs them for maintaining good health; those fats required for healthy biological processes.

floor barre (n.): A series of ballet warm-up exercises based on a traditional ballet *barre* routine executed while lying flat on the floor without the support of an actual bar.

freelancer (n.): Someone who is self-employed and not committed full-time to a term with an employer; an independent contractor.

glutamine (n.): An amino acid that may be considered conditionally essential in intensive athletic training; the most abundant naturally occurring amino acid in the body, found circulating in the blood and stored in skeletal muscles.

Graham, Martha (1894–1991): A highly regarded and influential American modern dancer and choreographer who developed her own technique based on the concept of contraction and release, focus on the center of the body, coordination between breath and movement, and a dancer's relationship with the floor.

grand jeté (n.): A French ballet term used to name the large jump in which a dancer's legs split apart in the air.

guesting ("gig") (n.): A temporary performing or teaching engagement in which a dancer is contracted as a guest artist.

Gyrokinesis (n.): A training method developed by Juliu Horvath, which has the same basic principles as gyrotonics, but most exercises are done while seated on a special stool as opposed to on machinery, as in gyrotonics.

Gyrotonics (n.): A training method developed by Juliu Horvath that is extremely complementary to a dancer's training; using exercises, done in a circular motion on an apparatus, to develop strength and stability of the core, back, legs, arms, and hips. It is also quite beneficial in helping to improve one's general flexibility.

hyponatremia (n.): An electrolyte disturbance usually caused as a result of excess water accumulating in the body at a higher rate than it can be excreted, thereby diluting essential sodium in the body; may be a result of overhydration.

individual retirement account (IRA) (n.): A type of retirement plan that provides tax advantages for retirement savings in the United States.

interest (n.): The extra money earned over time by funds that are deposited into a specified account or fund.

invest (v.): To put money into something with the expectation of a gain, which normally has a high degree of security for the initial (principal) amount and a reasonable security of return over an expected period of time.

kettlebell training (n.): A specialized weight training method that uses momentum and the swinging of kettlebells (cannonball-shaped weights with a curved handle).

mutual fund (n.): A type of professionally managed collective investments method that pools together money from a number of different investors to purchase securities (banknotes, bonds, stocks, etc.).

orthopedic physician (n.): A doctor who specializes in diagnosing and treating problems of the musculoskeletal system (muscles, joints, bones, ligaments, tendons, and nerves).

per diem (n.): A specified amount of money, an allowance, that an organization gives an individual to cover travel, living, and food expenses while working away from home or on tour.

Pilates (n.): A physical fitness and conditioning program developed by Joseph Pilates, also known as contrology; based primarily on the idea of building muscle awareness and control, all exercises are done with the muscles working to lift against gravity and the resistance of springs.

pirouette (n.): The French ballet term used to mean "turn." Several different types of pirouettes can be done in varied positions.

plié (n.): A step that is a smooth and continuous bending of the knees.

premier danseur (n.): The French term meaning "first dancer." It is the title given to principal male dancers, equivalent to the woman's title of prima ballerina.

pro rate (v.): To calculate, divide, and spread one's total yearly salary over a determined period of time longer than the actual weeks of employment stated in a contract.

relevé (n.): A motion during which one rises up from any position to balance on one foot or both with heels elevated off the floor.

tax (n.): An enforced, involuntary contribution of a portion of one's earnings to the government, imposed and regulated by the government.

Vaganova method (n.): The ballet technique and training system developed by Russian dancer Agrippina Vaganova that fuses elements of traditional romantic-era French technique with the athleticism and virtuosity of the Italian school. The method is designed to work the body as a whole, increase awareness of the body, and create a harmony of movement and great expressive range. The training regime is complex and rigorously planned.

Certified Medical Contributors

RYAN SOBUS, MPH, RD

Co-owner of Healthy Diets, Inc. and a registered member of the Academy of Nutrition and Dietetics, Ryan Sobus earned her master of public health nutrition degree from the University of North Carolina at Chapel Hill, and her bachelor of science degree in biology from Converse College. As a competitive runner, she learned from an early age what a powerful grip disordered eating could have on her teammates. She has positioned herself to be an expert in the field of dietetics to help others develop a healthy relationship with food. She believes that everyone deserves to be healthy and has the ability to achieve it—with the awareness and motivation to take care of our bodies.

MICHELLE KHAI, BS, CSCS

A multi-dimensional movement specialist, Michelle Khai received her professional dance training at Alvin Ailey American Dance Theater. Her specialty is in performance enhancement and injury prevention for dancers. Khai was one of the creators of Kettle-bell Concepts and served as the chief science officer and master instructor. She has been certified as an NCSA strength and conditioning specialist, an American College of Sports Medicine health fitness instructor, and as a medical exercise specialist.

CYNTHIA MCGEE LAPORTILLA, MSPT, LMT

Miami City Ballet senior physical therapist Cynthia McGee Laportilla is the head of MCB's physiotherapy department and is a board-certified physical therapist and massage therapist, specializing in sports and dance medicine.

MILLIE FIGUEREDO, PHD

A specialist in clinical psychology, Dr. Millie Figueredo runs a private practice in South Miami and volunteers her services to help the dancers and students of Miami City Ballet on an ongoing basis. A devoted and loving mother of two professional ballerinas, she is able to sympathize with the challenges that young dancers encounter on a daily basis and is dedicated to helping them reach their career goals in the healthiest and happiest way possible.

Index

Jennifer Carlynn Kronenberg was born in Queens, New York, where she trained with Teresa Aubel, Nicholas Orloff, Norman Walker, and Barbara Walczack. She continued her studies on scholarship at the School of American Ballet before joining Miami City Ballet as an apprentice in 1994 at the age of seventeen. She moved steadily through the ranks and was named principal dancer in 2001. She danced at the Kennedy Center Honors in 1997 and at the Jacob's Pillow and Aspen festivals, Torino Danza Festival in Italy, the Kennedy Center's International Ballet Festival, the Vail International Dance Festival, and most recently at the New York City Center's Fall for Dance performance series. In July 2011 she was featured on PBS's *Great Performances* in "Dance in America: Miami City Ballet Dances Balanchine and Tharp." She has also been featured on numerous occasions in *Pointe* Magazine, *Dance ViewTimes*, and *Dance Spirit* Magazine. She wrote the essay "From the Heart: Why I Dance" for *Dance* Magazine's April 2011 issue. Ms. Kronenberg has been a regular teacher for the Miami City Ballet Summer Intensive Program for the last several years and has also been a guest teacher with El Ballet de Monterrey Curso de Verano, New Orleans Center for Creative Arts, Ballet Chicago, and Ballet Arts of Jackson, Tennessee, among many others.

The University Press of Florida is the scholarly publishing agency for the State University System of Florida, comprising Florida A&M University, Florida Atlantic University, Florida Gulf Coast University, Florida International University, Florida State University, New College of Florida, University of Central Florida, University of Florida, University of North Florida, University of South Florida, and University of West Florida.